Direct Election of the President

Direct Election of the President

Harvey Zeidenstein
Illinois State University

Lexington Books
D.C. Heath and Company
Lexington, Massachusetts
Toronto   London

Library of Congress Cataloging in Publication Data

Zeidenstein, Harvey G.
  Direct election of the President.

  1. Presidents—United States—Election. I. Title.
JK528.Z43   324'.24   73-1135
ISBN 0-669-86116-2

Published simultaneously in Canada.

Printed in the United States of America.

International Standard Book Number: 0-669-86116-2

Library of Congress Catalog Card Number: 73-1135

To my parents

Contents

List of Tables

Acknowledgments

Various institutions and individuals have contributed, directly or indirectly, to the publication of this book. Illinois State University granted me the time and financial aid without which this study would still be "in the works." Alberta Carr, typist and grammarian *par excellence*, literally removed the blots from my copy book. Bill Day and Bill Hey of the Illinois Legislative Council, good friends and exacting editors in years past, officiated at the marriage of journalistic clarity and scholarly objectivity. Finally, given the constricted market for monographs, any first-time author who does not thank his publisher is either a fool or an ingrate.

Direct Election of the President

Part I
The Electoral College and the Direct Vote Alternative

1

Legislative Background: The Issue Raised, The Decision Deferred

During the last three weeks of September 1970, the activities of the United States Senate were punctuated by periods of extended debate on Senate Joint Resolution 1—a proposal to amend the Constitution by abolishing the Electoral College and replacing it with direct popular election of the President. Sponsored by Senator Birch Bayh, chairman of the subcommittee on constitutional amendments of the Judiciary Committee, S.J. Res. 1 was substantively similar to H.J. Res. 681, which had passed the House by an overwhelming vote of 339-70 a year earlier.

Both resolutions established a minimum of 40 percent of the popular vote as sufficient to elect a President and Vice-President running as a team. If no candidate polled a 40 percent plurality, a runoff election would be held between the two top vote-getters. Despite favorable action in the House, the Senate never brought S.J. Res. 1 to a vote. Two attempts to close debate by cloture failed, the second and last on September 29th. That marked the end of electoral reform for the 91st Congress.[1]

The Senate debate, which began on September 8th, was preceded by three days of hearings before the Senate Judiciary Committee in mid-April and by the Committee's favorable report on S.J. Res. 1, filed on August 14th.[2] The fascinating aspect of the report's minority views and of the Senate debate is that while the proposal was roundly attacked by conservative Senators, much of their ammunition was manufactured in a liberal arsenal. Time and again, Senators James O. Eastland, Sam J. Ervin, Roman L. Hruska, Carl T. Curtis, and J. Strom Thurmond assailed S.J. Res. 1 by quoting extensively from the writings and hearings testimony of such liberals as law professor Alexander Bickel, former presidential aide and political activist Richard Goodwin, and journalist Theodore White, among others. This curious shift was complemented by proponents of direct election, who cited the support of such normally conservative groups as the American Bar Association and the U.S. Chamber of Commerce, as well as of President Nixon.

The terms "liberal" and "conservative" are not used to designate opposing positions on the unidimensional issue of direct election. Rather, these terms denote, in a rough sense, the overall policy posture and public image of various actors and interest groups on such issues as civil rights, social welfare programs, the role of the federal government in managing the economy, and the pace and manner of ending the war in Vietnam. Although not all political actors have taken a position on all these issues, it is probably fair to say that Senators

3

Hruska, Curtis, Eastland, Thurmond, and Ervin, and the U.S. Chamber of Commerce, can be classified as "conservative." Senators Birch Bayh, Jacob Javits, Alexander Bickel, and Richard Goodwin can be classified as "liberal."[3] Yet Bayh and Javits support the principle of direct election; Bickel and Goodwin adamantly oppose it.

Indeed, Bickel and Goodwin not only testified against direct election, they also utilized the pages of liberal publications to warn fellow liberals that advocating direct election would bring them political oblivion.[4]

The purpose of this study is to critically examine the argument that direct election of the President will have dire and dysfunctional consequences for the nation in general and for liberal groups in particular. Chapter 2 presents the charges against the Electoral College as it currently operates, along with some rebuttal against such charges. It then outlines the case for direct election of the President and concludes with a brief summary of the provisions and pitfalls of three other proposals for electoral reform. With the foundation established in Chapter 2, Chapters 3 through 6 analyze in depth the predicted dysfunctional consequences of direct election. The mode of analysis is twofold: (1) explicating the premises upon which the predicted consequences are based and considering the reasonableness of these premises, and (2) offering such empirical evidence as is available which bears on the validity of the premises, the predicted consequences, or both. The final chapter will summarize conclusions drawn from the preceding analysis in the context of recommending change in our electoral system, in order of priority.

Notes

1. On January 28, 1971, Senator Bayh introduced a revised version of his amendment, also titled S.J. Res. 1, for the 1st session of the 92nd Congress. This resolution was not reported out of committee.

2. Hearings before the Senate Judiciary Committee on ELECTORAL COLLEGE REFORM, 91st Cong., 2nd Sess. (April 15, 16, and 17, 1970), hereafter cited as Senate Hearings, and Senate Report No. 91-1123, 91st Cong., 2nd Sess., Judiciary Committee, "Direct Popular Election of the President" (August 14, 1970).

3. There are always exceptions to broad generalizations. Senator Ervin, for example, is probably second to no one in his championship of individual civil liberties and procedural due process. But as a Southerner, his liberalism does not extend to civil rights for blacks.

4. See, e.g., Alexander Bickel, "Direct Election of the President," THE NEW REPUBLIC (September 26, 1970), and "The Case for the Electoral College," THE NEW REPUBLIC (January 28, 1967), and Richard Goodwin, "Electoral College: Best Way? Direct Election Has Its Faults," WASHINGTON POST, October 5, 1969, reprinted in Senate Hearings, 99-101 and in 116 CONG. REC. S15216-17 (daily ed., September 11, 1970).

2
Electoral Vote Versus Popular Vote

An axiom of democratic theory is that reasonable men may reasonably differ. But since this is not a universal law, it follows that occasionally reasonable men may differ unreasonably. Few issues offer better examples of the axiom and its exception than the electoral vote versus popular vote controversy.

By and large, men disagree for two kinds of reasons. They may assign different weights to a given value—in this case, the principle of equality as implemented through an electoral mechanism assuring one-man, one-vote. They may differ also in their perceptions of the relative probability of a given consequence occurring, the degree of harm or benefit ensuing from such a consequence, or both. Those who disagree over the utility of the Electoral College are motivated by both categories of conflict.

The Case Against the Electoral College: Values

The sharpest thrust against the Electoral College is that it violates a primary democratic value—that in selecting from among alternatives, each person's vote should be equal to every other person's vote. The distribution of the electoral vote rarely coincides with the distribution of the popular vote, for three reasons.

First, there is the distortion effected by the "constant two" senatorial electors awarded each state and the District of Columbia regardless of its population. These 102 electoral votes constitute about 19 percent of all electoral votes. They represent 51 jurisdictional units on the map, not people.

The second cause of disparity between electoral and popular votes is that each state casts a set number of electoral votes regardless of the number of people who go to the polls. In the 1960 election, for example, 25.5 percent of the adult citizens of Mississippi voted for President. Each electoral vote represented 37,271 voters. Yet Kansas, with the same number of electoral votes, had a popular vote turnout of 70.3 percent, for a ratio of 116,103 popular votes to each electoral vote. Nor is this an isolated example. In 1968 the national turnout was about 61 percent of the voting-age population. In five states, fewer than 50 percent of the voting-age population voted; in 20 states, less than 60 percent; and in nine states, more than 70 percent.

The unit rule provision, whereby the winner of a plurality of a state's popular vote is awarded all of that state's electoral votes, is the third and most severe violation of the one-man, one-vote principle.[1] Those who vote for a losing candidate fail to have their votes reflected in the awarding of a state's electoral votes. But the inequity does not stop there. A state receives one electoral vote for each of its congressional seats, and the number of seats are roughly in proportion to a state's total population. Since those who vote for a losing candidate are part of their state's population, the unit rule, in effect, transmutes their popular votes against the winning candidate into electoral votes for him.

Although this phenomenon is sometimes astounding to those who first learn of it, personal experience bears testimony that virtually all students in introductory political science courses "get the picture." The same, unfortunately, cannot always be said for far more learned people whose opposition to direct election seems based on an intellectual blind spot. Consider the following dialogue between Senator Ervin and Charles Black, Henry Luce Professor of Jurisprudence, Yale Law School:[2]

Senator Ervin. I used to be much concerned about the fact that in the state, the man who voted for the second candidate or third, fourth, or fifth, his vote was not counted. But sort of meditating on the federal system, I feel as you stated a while ago, that there are some things you cannot explain why it works or why we get this strength in the Constitution. Reflecting on that, I do not think that is too bad.

Mr. Black. I do not, either, because if Mr. Banzhaf's mathematics are right, if the calculations of practical people in politics for decades have been right, the man in the large state who has relatively less representation in the Senate will at least be attended to with respect to the next election more than elsewhere, and this effect of which I spoke, this compensating effect, would work out as to him.

Another thing, of course: *Somebody always loses his vote, somebody wins. You could argue that the man who votes for a loser in a congressional race loses his vote. The winner takes all in that case.* [Emphasis added.]

Senator Ervin. Yes.

Mr. Black. I think the concept of your vote being lost has been insufficiently thought to the depths, perhaps, *because if you lose, you always lose your vote in a sense, but you have had a chance to win it.* [Emphasis added.]

Senator Ervin. I am glad you made that observation, because I think it is a sound observation, and does away with the conclusion that it is a great tragedy, because *he certainly loses if he votes for the losing candidate for Governor or for any other office.* [Emphasis added.]

Mr. Black. Right, and you have to decide whether this compensating effect is, which prevails with the winner take all system, is enough to justify this. My conclusion would be that it is.

This reasoning is so muddled that one hardly knows where to begin setting it straight. First, and most obviously, Professor Black equates as similar two quite different meanings of the concept "winner takes all" (and, by inference, its opposite entailment that "losers win nothing"). In the context of congressional and gubernatorial elections, the concept means that the candidate with a plurality of popular votes in a given constituency wins the one and only *elective office* for which all candidates are running. With only one, indivisible prize available, by definition the winner "takes all." But a state's electoral votes are not synonymous with the office sought. They are instrumental units of measure for winning the Presidency, just as popular votes are units of measure for winning all other elective offices in the nation. Moreover, electoral votes are a *divisible* prize. Only because of the unit rule does the winner of a popular vote plurality "take all" of them.

This is basic, almost primitive. But the mischief of the Black-Ervin thesis is that it ignores simple, generic differences. An individual's vote is an official, personal *expression of choice* from among candidates for office. The winner is determined by counting the number of expressed choices for each candidate and awarding the office to the candidate with the greater number. So long as one's vote is *counted for the candidate of one's choice*, that vote is not "lost." That candidate may not have a number of votes sufficient to win, but there is surely a world of difference between a *losing candidate* and a lost *vote* for that candidate. Assuming each valid vote is given equal weight in the count, a vote can be "lost" only in one of two ways. It can be ignored, or it can be added to the votes for a candidate who is not one's choice. The latter adds insult to injury, for the vote is not only "lost" for the candidate of one's choice but "found" for the candidate one opposes.

Assuming an honest and accurate count, in elections for congressman, governor, or senator, votes are not officially ignored or counted for the candidate against whom a person has voted. A popular vote is an expression of personal, individual choice. It is concrete. An electoral vote is an expression of impersonal, collective choice. It is abstract. Only the abstraction of electoral votes intervening between voter and candidate, coupled with the unit rule, makes legal in the structure of presidential elections what would be considered fraud in all other elections in the nation.

There remains what Professor Black calls the "compensating effect" of residing in a large state. Although what is being compensated for is by no means clear, Black seems to be saying that although the citizen of the large state "has relatively less representation in the Senate" than the citizen of the small state, this disparity of *legislative* representation is compensated for in terms of greater *executive* representation in the person of the President.

There are at least two faults with this argument. First, it is irrelevant to the point raised by Senator Ervin.[3] The issue is not equal numbers of Senators per state, or even the "constant two" electors resulting from them. It is that in all states with the unit rule, small as well as large, voting choices of electoral minorities are counted for the plurality candidate. This happens in Nevada as well as New York. The bone of contention is a matter of intra-state voter inequality, not inter-state jurisdictional inequality. Professor Black is worrying the wrong bone.

The second fault is that even if the issue were one of inter-state inequality, to date there is no theoretical or operational way of measuring (no less equating) disparities of *numerical representation in a collective body*, such as the Senate, with differences in the probability of determining the *outcome of an election*, especially to the single office of the Presidency. These are two different phenomena. It is true that by making certain mathematical gaming assumptions, Banzhaf finds that under the Electoral College unit-rule system, the individual voter in a large state has a greater *relative* probability of casting the deciding vote for President than does the individual voter in a small state.[4] But Professor Black offers no clear common denominator between this and representation in the Senate.

The Case Against the Electoral College: Consequences

Violation of the principle of equal weight for each popular vote does not exist in a philosophical limbo. Opponents of the Electoral College charge that it has had and could have dire consequences in the real political world. In order of their probable severity, the consequences are: (1) the election of a candidate who comes in second in the popular vote; (2) failing a majority in the Electoral College, there would be secret bargaining for the Presidency, which could also result in electing a minority candidate; (3) two-party competition is inhibited in one-party states; (4) the unit rule encourages fraud in counting the popular vote in states with large blocs of electoral votes; and (5) an elector may not vote for the candidate who carried his state. All but the third and fifth consequences are dependent on a close election, measured in terms of popular votes.

Electing a Minority Candidate

There is historical evidence that at least twice, in 1876 and 1888, the nation elected a President who ran second in popular votes.[5] Statistical evidence indicates that we have come close to electing minority Presidents in the recent past, and may very likely do so in the near future.

In 1876 Samuel J. Tilden received 251,000 more votes than Rutherford B. Hayes, or 50.99 percent to Hayes' 48.04 percent. But allegations of widespread fraud led to an investigation by a 15-member commission. Splitting along partisan lines, by an 8 to 7 vote the commission awarded all the disputed electoral votes to Hayes, who then received 185 electoral votes to Tilden's 184.

In 1888 Grover Cleveland's plurality over Benjamin Harrison exceeded 95,000 votes, or 48.66 percent to Harrison's 47.86 percent. Yet because he lost New York by about 13,000 votes out of the 1.3 million votes cast in that state, Cleveland received but 168 electoral votes to Harrison's 233.

The Electoral College has come close to electing a runner-up in recent years. Although Truman had a 2.2 million popular vote plurality over Dewey in 1948, and a seemingly comfortable electoral vote margin of 303 to Dewey's 189, a shift of less than 30,000 votes in Illinois, California, and Ohio would have made Dewey President. Similarly, a shift of less than 12,000 votes, properly distributed among five states, would have elected Nixon over Kennedy in 1960. "In fact," writes Neal Peirce, "only sheer luck has saved the nation from the choice of the popular-vote loser in the electoral college in several recent elections."[6]

Some rough probabilities of electing a minority President emerge from a statistical analysis of presidential elections by Charles Bischoff of MIT.

The experience of the past 50 years, Bischoff concluded, shows that in an election as close as that between Kennedy and Nixon [Kennedy's plurality was about 112,000 votes], there is no better than a 50-50 chance that the electoral vote will agree with the popular vote as to the winner. When the leading candidate has a plurality of about 500,000 (or 0.57 percent, based on a 70-million-vote turnout), the verdict would still be reversed about one time in three. [Nixon's 1968 plurality over Humphrey was 510,000 votes out of 73 million.] ... Projected 40 years hence (to the election of 2008), when the voter turnout will probably be at least 140 million, even a 1-million-vote plurality will fail to elect the popular vote winner in one election out of three.[7]

Bargaining for the Presidency

In a close election between major party candidates, if a third party or a slate of unpledged electors wins a handful of electoral votes, this could deny any candidate a majority of electoral votes needed to win the Presidency. Should this happen, the Constitution provides that the Senate shall elect the Vice-President from the top two candidates and the House of Representatives shall elect the President from among the top three electoral vote winners, each state's delegation casting one vote, regardless of the population of the state. Should a delegation be unable to decide by majority vote whom to vote for, that delegation would not even cast its single vote.

The opportunities for bargaining in the House are self-evident. If a majority of House delegations are controlled by the party whose presidential candidate comes in second in the popular vote, the electoral vote, or both, the House could very easily "elect" a minority President.

Chilling as this prospect may be, it could be preempted by third party (or unpledged) electors bargaining with one or both major party candidates for their votes, thus assuring that a major party candidate will receive a majority of electoral votes. The 40-odd days between the election and the casting of electoral votes in state capitols offers ample time for such "balance of power" electors to throw their support to the highest bidder.

Although the Electoral College has always yielded a majority in every election since 1824, there have been three close calls just since World War II. In the four-way election of 1948, Truman won 303 electoral votes, Dewey 189, and Dixiecrat J. Strom Thurmond 39. But a switch from Truman to Dewey of less than 13,000 popular votes in California and Ohio would have deprived both major party candidates of an electoral vote majority, although Truman would still have had 2 million more popular votes than Dewey. Thurmond's 39 electors could have carried the day for either candidate.[8]

The price to Truman presumably would have been renunciation of the strong civil rights plank in the Democratic platform which prompted the Dixiecrat movement. Failing Truman's capitulation, Dewey might have had the 39 electors by continuing to hold to his vague campaign positions.

Kennedy's eyelash victory over Nixon in 1960 might also have turned on the kind of bargaining typical of an oriental bazaar. Kennedy's 303 to 219 electoral-vote margin obscures the fact that a popular vote shift of about 9,400 votes in Illinois and Missouri would have shifted the 38 electoral votes of those states from Kennedy to Nixon, leaving Kennedy four votes short of a majority and Nixon 12 votes short. The 14 unpledged electors from Mississippi and Alabama (plus one Republican elector from Oklahoma who voted for Senator Harry Byrd of Virginia) would, again, have put Southern electors in a bargaining, balance-of-power position. But given the South's animosity toward Kennedy's religion[9] (which presumably was not negotiable), it is questionable whether they would have even attempted to bargain with him. The greater likelihood would have been unilateral negotiations with Nixon to forestall throwing the election into the House.

George Wallace's candidacy in 1968 seemed clearly intended to put him, and his electors, in a bargaining position if neither major party candidate won a majority in the Electoral College. In an interview published in a national magazine early in the campaign, Wallace was asked if, failing an electoral majority for anyone, two candidates would get together, or their electors would get together, and determine who would become President? Wallace reportedly responded, "That is right."[10]

Although Nixon's 301 electoral votes foreclosed such a possibility, they allowed a scant margin of safety. A shift of less than 43,000 votes from Nixon to Humphrey in Missouri, New Jersey, and Alaska would have deprived Nixon of 32 electoral votes and left him one vote short of a majority. Similarly, a shift of something over 55,000 votes in Ohio and Missouri would have cost him 38 electoral votes, seven short. Wallace's 46 electors (including one North Carolina Republican who defected) would have easily put Nixon over the top—for a price.

Writing speculative historical scenarios is always a chancy enterprise. The above examples are no exception. They presuppose just the right shift of popular votes in just the right states to entail the possible gloomy outcomes. Defenders of the status quo can point to history and say "It didn't happen." Proponents of change charge that it could have. To allow continuation of a reasonable threat is to think like the proverbial Arkansas woodchopper, who never patched the hole in his roof because on rainy days he would get wet and on dry days the roof didn't leak.

Inhibiting Two-Party Competition

The unit rule is assailed as damming the tide of two-party competition from reaching traditional one-party states. Since Republican candidates cannot win any electoral votes in Democratic states and Democratic candidates cannot carry Republican states, such states are ignored by the presidential candidate of the minority party. Indeed, Senator Howard Baker, Republican of Tennessee, took the Senate floor to charge that his state had been ignored by both parties; by Democrats because they "had it in the bag," and by Republicans because they thought they couldn't carry the state, despite a large minority of Republican voters.

Such charges were blunted by Senator Spesser Holland, Democrat of Florida. He presented presidential voting statistics for the South for the elections of 1956 through 1968 to bolster his argument that the South has had healthy competition.

On balance, it is probably reasonable to conclude that the unit rule inhibits as much competition for the vote as there might be, but that the erosion of one-party states has promoted more competition than there used to be.

Encouraging Fraudulent Vote Counts

Populous states with large blocs of electoral votes tend to divide their popular votes closely between the two parties. Consequently, because of the unit rule, a fraudulent count of a few thousand votes can shift the entire bloc of a state's electoral votes from one candidate to another. The relatively low risk (stealing a few thousand votes in one or two counties) for a high payoff (winning a score or more of electoral votes) can be particularly inviting in a close contest for a majority of the Electoral College. Fraud in one or two states can tip a close national election one way or the other.

Faithless Electors

Opponents of the Electoral College attribute moral fraud to a Republican or Democratic elector who does not vote for the candidate of his party. There are no legal sanctions for preventing or punishing such "faithless" electors. However, from 1820 through 1968, only nine of more than 15,000 electoral votes have been cast contrary to instructions. In no case has a faithless elector changed the outcome of an election.

The Case for Direct Election

After so detailed a critique of the Electoral College, advocates of direct election sum up their case in a straightforward manner:[11]

1. It is the only method which assures that the candidate with the most popular votes will win the election.

2. The *de facto* disenfranchisement of those who vote for a losing candidate would end. Each person's vote would count equally across the nation, being neither eclipsed nor magnified many times its weight by the chance factor of state residence. This, in turn, would have two desirable consequences. There would be greater two-party competition for the vote in traditional one-party states, and party organizations in all states would be encouraged to get all potential voters registered and to the polls.

3. Regionally-based splinter parties or unpledged electors would be denied an opportunity to throw the election into the House, or to solicit concessions from major party candidates in return for their electoral votes.

4. Localized corruption in a single state would be far less likely to determine the outcome of a national election than under the Electoral College, unit-rule system.

5. There would no longer be human electors who could vote contrary to the intent of a plurality or a majority of the voters in their state.

6. Direct election is overwhelmingly favored by the public in all sections of the nation. Recent Gallup surveys find that 76 percent of respondents in the South are favorable, and from 81 to 82 percent of the people in the East, the Midwest, and the West support direct election.[12]

The Runoff

A runoff election, contingent upon no candidate polling at least 40 percent of the popular vote, is the most controversial part of the direct vote proposal. Critics argue that it would become a self-fulfilling condition. If there were a runoff, minor party candidates could extract promises from the major party candidates in exchange for throwing their voting support to them. But a runoff is possible only if there are enough minor party votes to deny 40 percent to a major party candidate. Minor parties would, therefore, form with this express purpose in mind. Having formed, they would accomplish their purpose. Q.E.D., allowing a runoff is a necessary and sufficient condition to cause a runoff.

The empirical assumptions of this, and related arguments, will be probed in some detail in later chapters. Suffice to say, at this point, that the 40 percent/runoff contingency election can be defended as follows:

1. The 40 percent plurality figure is a compromise. A President who receives less than 40 percent of the vote would have an insufficient mandate to govern. A President who receives more would not. The 40 percent figure allows minor parties to win up to 20 percent of the vote without triggering the runoff contingency. Since minor parties are unlikely to win this many votes, they would be dissuaded from trying. The two-party tradition would be preserved.

2. In the remote possibility that a contingency election is necessary, the runoff is the only type that permits the people to choose their national leader.

Alternative to the Runoff: Election by Congress

The runoff is preferable to a contingent election in Congress because the runoff assures that the popular choice between the top two candidates will be elected. Election by Congress does not.

Nearly all supporters of the electoral vote principle concede the undesirability of a contingency election in the House, with each state casting one vote for one of the top three presidential candidates, and election of the Vice-President in the Senate. They are joined by some who favor direct election on the first ballot, but who also oppose a popular vote runoff.

The contingency plan that appears to have emerging support is a joint session of the newly elected Congress in which each member votes individually for one of the top two presidential and vice-presidential tickets. These would be either the top two tickets in electoral votes or in popular votes, depending on the form of election used on the first ballot.

The minimal change proposed for amending the Constitution, the so-called Katzenbach or automatic plan, would abolish human electors, automatically award all the electoral votes of a state to the winner of a popular vote plurality in each state, and send the election to a joint session of Congress if no candidate receives a majority of electoral votes.[13]

Election by Congress is also the last-ditch proviso of an amendment to S.J. Res. 1 offered by Senator Robert Griffin and former Senator Joseph Tydings in 1970.[14] Under the Griffin-Tydings plan, a candidate who wins at least a 40 percent plurality of the popular vote would be elected. If no candidate receives 40 percent, but the candidate with a plurality of the popular vote also wins a majority of electoral votes—with the votes cast automatically under the unit rule in each state—that candidate would be elected. If no candidate leads in the popular vote and wins a majority of the electoral vote, the runoff is held in a joint session of Congress, which selects from among the two candidates with the highest popular vote.

Senator Bayh's 1971 version of direct election, also numbered S.J. Res. 1, abolishes the runoff provision of his 1970 bill and replaces it with the Griffin-Tydings plan. In effect, this makes the automatic plan the first-stage contingency election (with the important modification that the electoral vote winner must also be a popular vote winner) and election in Congress the second stage contingency.

As a supporter of the automatic plan, Bickel favors a contingency election in Congress. He reasons that absence of an electoral vote majority constitutes deadlock. "Deadlock means that the coalition-making exercise which takes place before the general election has failed and must be tried again. Coalition-making is a function for representative, deliberative institutions. Congress sitting in joint session and reaching decisions by a majority of the individual votes of its members is the best available deliberative institution for this purpose at such a time. . . ."[15] Eschewing the "deliberative" role for Congress, Sayre and Parris assume that with only the top two candidates to choose from, "the vote would almost surely be along straight party lines, permitting very little discretion on the part of individual members of Congress."[16]

Neither argument is persuasive. Election by Congress strips a President of a good deal of his independence from *legislative* wheeling and dealing and from immense pressures to make him indebted to those legislators who voted for him. This kind of indebtedness differs from that incurred with convention delegates or the electorate, in that the President's congressional creditors are (1) constantly on hand to demand payment by way of policy outputs and administrative policy outcomes, and (2) are full-time political actors who interact with the President at the federal level. With these kinds of payoffs in the offing, when Bickel labels the electoral process in Congress "deliberation" he is being highly charitable.

But more importantly, Bickel rings in Congress unnecessarily because he fails to distinguish between the poles of two separate dimensions of coalition decision-making. One dimension relates to the number of options available—whether a choice must be winnowed from among several options or only two. The first case requires more deliberation, and is found in such roughly representative, deliberative institutions as nominating conventions and legislative bodies. But when the options boil down to the two top presidential candidates, the electorate can make the choice as easily as Congress, and far more democratically. The second dimension encompasses the nature or domain of the choice. Determining substantive public policy constitutes one domain, selecting government officials who will determine policy is another. In the context of American constitutionalism, the first domain is in the province of legislative bodies, the second belongs to the electorate.

Sayre and Parris's assumption that Congress would elect the President on a straight party-line vote is probably naïve. But if they were right, it could mean that the winner of a popular plurality or an electoral vote plurality could lose the election if he were a member of the minority party in Congress. After the close 1968 election there were 300 Democrats and 235 Republicans in Congress. A straight party line vote would have elected Humphrey, despite the fact that the election could have gone to Congress with Nixon still holding a plurality of nearly a half-million popular votes.

Even Richard Goodwin, an opponent of direct election, prefers a popular vote runoff to allowing Congress the "privilege of selecting a minority candidate."

Of course, a "minority" President, or a majority President with his legislative program severely constrained, could be elected because Congress does *not* vote exclusively by party affiliation. Consider, for example, legislators with "independent positions," defined as those whose states or congressional districts are carried by third party candidates such as George Wallace. In 1968 there were 58 "independent" members of Congress, compared to 231 Republicans and 246 Democrats whose constituencies were carried by one of the major party candidates.[17] Had the 1968 election been sent to a joint session of Congress, neither party would have achieved the necessary 268 vote majority without at least some of the "Wallaceite" votes. To suggest such votes would have been cast according to the legislator's nominal major party affiliation, without promises in return, is naïve. If nothing else, such legislators could have pleaded reprisals at their own next election if they failed to exact some measures pleasing to their Wallaceite constituency in return for their votes. That such pleadings would, in most cases, have been tongue-in-cheek rationalizations of personal preferences is beside the point.

Or consider another, more genuine type of cross-pressured member of Congress—members of one major party whose constituency has voted for the presidential candidate of the other major party. They, too, might be sorely tempted to cross party lines in balloting for the President, whether out of personal conviction or fear of electoral reprisal at the next election. Congressmen who narrowly won their own elections would certainly fall into the latter category. Excluding the 54 Democrats and 4 Republicans whose constituencies were carried by Wallace, 135 members of the 91st Congress (97 Democrats and 38 Republicans) would have been subjected to this partisan versus constituency cross-pressure. (See Table 2-1, rows 2 and 5.) Without their vote, the distribution of which is not predictable, neither candidate would have reached the 268-vote majority of a joint session with all members voting. (See Table 2-1, rows 3 and 6.) If we add to these 135 legislators the 58 from Wallaceite constituencies, "a total of 193 members [36 percent of the total membership of Congress] would have had to make the difficult choice between supporting their party's candidate or registering the revealed wishes of their constituencies for another party's candidate."

Only if *every* member of Congress ignored his party affiliation and voted for the major party candidate who carried his constituency, with legislators from

Table 2-1
Membership of 91st Congress, by Partisan Affiliation and by Major Party Presidential Candidate Carrying the Constituency

							Total	
(1) House Democrats	=	243	+	Senate Democrats	57	=	300 Democrats	(1)
(2) Nixon CDs[a]		$\dfrac{-66}{177}$	+	Nixon state	$\dfrac{-31}{26}$	=	$\dfrac{-97}{203}$ Cross-pressured Democrats	(2)
(3) Sure Democrats	=	177	+	Sure Democrats	26	=	203 Sure Democrats	(3)
(4) House Republicans	=	192	+	Senate Republicans	43	=	235 Republicans	(4)
(5) Humphrey CDs[a]		$\dfrac{-28}{164}$	+	Humphrey state	$\dfrac{-10}{33}$	=	$\dfrac{-38}{197}$ Cross-pressured Republicans	(5)
(6) Sure Republicans	=	164	+	Sure Republicans	33	=	197 Sure Republicans	(6)

Exhibit: If Voting for Major Party Candidate Carrying Constituency (Legislators from Wallace Constituencies Vote for Their Party's Candidate):

Nixon Votes	Humphrey Votes
164 House Republicans	177 House Democrats
66 House Democrats	28 House Republicans
33 Senate Republicans	26 Senate Democrats
31 Senate Democrats	10 Senate Republicans
Total $\overline{294}$	$\overline{241}$

[a]CDs = Congressional Districts

Source: Adapted from data in the source cited in note 17.

Wallaceite constituencies voting for their party's candidate, would Nixon have defeated Humphrey by 294 votes to 241. (See Table 2-1, Exhibit.) But this conformation would have been highly unlikely.

Election by a joint session of Congress opens a Pandora's box of ill-defined, shifting, multi-related variables lacking both predictive power and democratic characteristics. In 1970 a majority of the Senate Judiciary Committee rejected the Griffin-Tydings amendment to S.J. Res. 1 because:

The committee concluded that in the long run the political health of our democratic system would be strengthened if the final choice rests with the people. A choice by any body other than the people, it was felt, was either useless or mischievous—useless if it reflects the will of the people and mischievous if it does not.[18]

Other Proposals for Change

Over the years, Congress has entertained a variety of proposals for altering the existing structure of presidential elections. Two of these, the district plan and the proportional plan, would retain electoral votes but abolish the unit-rule principle for winning them. A third proposal, the federal system plan, would utilize popular votes and electoral votes, if necessary, to preclude a popular vote runoff. None of these schemes have mustered enough political support to make them of more than passing interest.

District Plan

The district plan requires each state legislature to create a number of single-elector districts equal to the number of U.S. Representatives from that state. Congressional districts could be used. The presidential candidate who wins a plurality of the popular vote in a district would receive the vote of its elector. The candidate with a plurality of the state-wide vote would win the two electoral votes representing the state's two U.S. Senators. The likelihood of faithless electors would be diminished by requiring electors to formally declare, before the election, who they intend to vote for. "Any vote cast by an elector contrary to the declaration made by him shall be counted as a vote cast in accordance with his declaration."[19] If no candidate wins a majority of the electoral votes, the newly elected Congress would meet in joint session to elect the President from the three candidates with the highest number of electoral votes. Election would be by majority vote with each member voting individually. Should Congress be unable to elect a candidate on the first four ballots, a fifth ballot would be limited to the top two candidates on the fourth ballot.

Proportional Plan

Under the proportional plan, human electors would be abolished, but states would retain their electoral votes.[20] Each presidential candidate would receive the same proportion of a state's electoral votes as his share of a state's popular vote. Recent versions of the plan provide that the candidate with the greatest number of electoral votes would be elected President, provided that number is at least 40 percent of all the electoral votes. Should no candidate reach a 40 percent plurality, a joint session of Congress would elect the President from the two candidates with the highest number of electoral votes.

Federal System Plan

The federal system plan, introduced by Senators Thomas F. Eagleton of Missouri and Robert Dole of Kansas, is a highly complex amalgam of direct election and the federalist principle of grouping votes by state.[21] The plan has three stages. In the first, a candidate would be elected if he wins a plurality of the national popular vote *and* pluralities *either* in more than half the states (including the District of Columbia) *or* in states that contain more than 50 percent of the total number of voters in the election. If the first stage fails to produce a winner, the second stage would be the Electoral College automatic plan—the unit rule without human electors. A majority of electoral votes would be sufficient for election. Should there still be no winner, the third stage would be triggered. It is a modified proportional plan. All but the two candidates with the greatest number of electoral votes would be eliminated, and the electoral votes which any of the eliminated candidates won in a state would be credited to the two leading candidates in proportion to their popular vote in that state. After redistributing the electoral votes of minor party candidates in this manner, the candidate with a majority of the electoral votes in the nation would be elected President.

Critique of Other Proposals

All three of these proposals are subject to a number of indictments, which vary according to the political predispositions of the advocate. The comment here will be from the perspective of those who favor direct election.

All three plans could elect a President who comes in second in the national popular vote. While this may be less likely than at present under the district plan and the proportional plan, because both eliminate the unit rule, both retain a minimum of three electoral votes in every state regardless of population (one elector for the U.S. Representative guaranteed each state in the Constitution, and the "constant two" senatorial electors). Also, in both proposals a state casts all its electoral votes regardless of how few voters may go to the polls. Voters in low turnout states would continue to exert disproportionate electoral influence compared to voters in states with high turnout. The district plan would allow the same corruption of voter equality *within* each state. The one electoral vote in, say, a low turnout, rural district would be equal to the electoral vote in a high turnout, suburban district. Inequality of voting power exerts even greater weight in the second stage of the federal district plan, for it retains the unit rule in awarding electoral votes. Finally, the election of a President with but 40 percent of the electoral vote, a provision of the proportional plan, would increase the probability of electing an "also ran" to the White House.

Both the proportional plan and the district plan would hold a contingency election in a joint session of Congress, the drawbacks of which have already been demonstrated.

By permitting state legislatures to draw the lines of electoral districts, the district plan is an open invitation to the most blatant kind of gerrymandering. Whether the districts were congressional districts or separate "presidential" districts, the dominant party in a state legislature would unquestionably attempt to compress the popular votes of the opposition party in as few districts as possible. Similarly, ethnic minorities might be the victims of gerrymandering in some states. Although the proposal requires that districts be composed of compact and contiguous territory, and be as equal in population as "practicable," these prohibitions would be of scant hindrance to a gerrymander. Appeal to the courts would be time-consuming at best, and may not even be permissible, for the district plan states that "such districts when formed shall not be altered until another census has been taken." Allowing the state legislatures so significant and untrammeled a role in structuring presidential elections constitutes the worst possible corruption of "federalism."

The camel has been called "a horse designed by a committee." The same observation applies to the federal system plan. The first stage elects a President with a plurality of popular votes (regardless of how small the plurality), providing he has demonstrated his wide geographic support by carrying any 26 states (a nod to the small states), or states with half the voters (a bribe to the large states). But the second and third stages revert back to the Electoral College, with all its appeal to so-called "federalists," its anathema to egalitarians, and its possibility of electing the second-place candidate. While the plan wisely keeps any contingent election out of Congress, it also prevents a popular vote majority by prohibiting a runoff between the two major party candidates. In attempting to satisfy too many conflicting demands, the plan is like a one-armed juggler trying to balance a set of rapidly melting snowballs. Finally, although it is ingenious in conception, the immense complexity in every stage of counting the vote makes the proposal politically unfeasible. Most citizens wouldn't understand how the President got into the White House.

Notes

1. In 1969, Maine adopted the district plan, providing that one elector shall be elected in each of Maine's two congressional districts and its "constant two" senatorial electors shall be elected at large. This opens the possibility that both parties may share Maine's electoral votes in a three to one split.

2. Hearings before the Senate Judiciary Committee on ELECTORAL COLLEGE REFORM, 91st Cong., 2nd Sess. (April 15, 16, and 17, 1970), 148. Hereafter cited as Senate Hearings.

3. Anyone familiar with Senator Ervin's record in Senate debate on this and other issues is not going to fault his intelligence. This writer strongly suspects that the dialogue between Ervin and Black is less a measure of the Senator's ability at ratiocination than of his political sagacity.

4. John F. Banzhaf III, "One Man, 3.312 Votes: A Mathematical Analysis of the Electoral College," VILLANOVA LAW REVIEW, 13 (Winter, 1968), 303-346. This article was subsequently reprinted in Hearings before the House Judiciary Committee on ELECTORAL COLLEGE REFORM, 91st Cong., 1st Sess. (1969), 309-352.

5. Some sources would add a third instance—the election of 1824 when Andrew Jackson won a plurality of both the popular and electoral vote in a four-way race, but lost to John Quincy Adams in the House of Representatives. This case should not be considered for a variety of reasons, not the least of which is that of the 24 states at that time, six (including New York, the most populous) did not yet have popular voting for presidential electors. For more complete grounds for exempting 1824 from consideration, see Appendix A to the minority views in Senate Report No. 91-1123, 91st Cong., 2nd Sess., Judiciary Committee, "Direct Popular Election of the President" (August 14, 1970), 52-54, hereafter cited as Senate Report.

6. Neil R. Peirce, THE PEOPLE'S PRESIDENT (New York: Simon and Schuster, 1968), 141.

7. Ibid., 142. Bischoff's study was commissioned for Peirce's book.

8. California and Ohio each had 25 electoral votes in 1948. Subtracting their 50 from Truman's 303 would have left him with 253, 13 short of a majority. Adding these 50 to Dewey's 189 would have given him 239, 27 short of a majority. Thurmond's 39 electoral votes were all either candidate would have needed.

9. Philip Converse and others, "Stability and Change in 1960: A Reinstating Election," AMERICAN POLITICAL SCIENCE REVIEW, 55 (June 1961), 269-280. See also the reports of private polling undertaken for Kennedy by Louis Harris and Associates, as reported in THE NEW YORK TIMES, February 18, 1962, 74.

10. U.S. NEWS AND WORLD REPORT, Sept. 30, 1968, quoted in Senate Report, 7.

11. Except where otherwise noted, the following is based on Peirce, PEOPLE'S PRESIDENT, 253-54, and remarks of Senator Jacob Javits in 116 CONG. REC. S15225 (daily ed., September 11, 1970).

12. Poll data cited by Senator Bayh in 116 CONG. REC. S14948 (daily ed., September 8, 1970).

13. Proposed by the Johnson Administration in 1966, through the auspices of the then Attorney General, Nicholas deB. Katzenbach. The 1970 version was introduced by Senator Sam J. Ervin, Jr. as S.J. Res. 191, 91st Cong., 2nd Sess.

14. See Senate Report, 20-21.

15. Alexander Bickel, REFORM AND CONTINUITY (New York: Harper Colophon Books, 1971), 34.

16. Wallace Sayre and Judith Parris, VOTING FOR PRESIDENT (Washington, D.C.: The Brookings Institution, 1970), 99. Note that Sayre and Parris do not advocate election of the President by joint session of Congress. They escape this position by opposing any constitutional change in the manner of electing the President. But that leaves a contingency election in the House.

17. These data, and other data on the partisan composition of the 91st Congress mentioned in the following two paragraphs, are taken from Joseph Kallenbach, "The Presidency and the Constitution: A Look Ahead," one article in a symposium on "The Institutionalized Presidency" published in LAW AND CONTEMPORARY PROBLEMS, 35 (Summer 1970), 445-460, at 458-59.

18. Senate Report, 13.

19. S.J. Res. 12, 91st Cong., 1st Sess. (1969).

20. The plan has been associated with its chief advocates in the late 1940s and 1950s, former Senator Henry Cabot Lodge of Massachusetts and former Representative Ed Gossett of Texas. Recent versions of the proposal have been sponsored by various Senators, including Senator Sam J. Ervin of North Carolina, who introduced it as S.J. Res. 2 in the 91st Cong., 1st Sess. (1969).

21. S.J. Res. 181, 91st Cong., 2nd Sess. (1970).

Part II
The Case Against Direct Election: Analysis and Rebuttal

3 Protecting Urban Interests— Myth or Reality?

Most students and practitioners of politics agree that the wellsprings of liberal electoral strength flow from the large, metropolitan states. Some liberals also assume that such states now have an electoral advantage in the Electoral College. They claim this advantage would be lost in a direct election of the President. The urban interests argument is composed of the following propositions, some explicit, some implicit.[1]

1. The direct vote plan abolishes electoral votes and the unit rule. This would eliminate the prize that the most populous states "can offer of a large bloc of [electoral] votes available to the highest bidder."

2. Because the popular vote for President tends to be close in the urban, populous states, a numerically small group which votes in a bloc can swing all the electoral votes of its state to one party or the other.

3. Such cohesive voting groups include racial and ethnic minorities dwelling in or near the large inner cities, such as blacks, Jews, the Irish, Puerto Ricans, and Italians. These groups are presumed to be "liberal" and *cohesive with each other* [implicit proposition], and cohesive with "progressive urban-suburban Republicans. . . . " In sum, there is a "metropolitan bloc" composed of "liberal, urban Democrats and progressive, urban-suburban Republicans [which has] tended to dominate presidential politics. . . . "

4. Because of the electoral clout of such cohesive, balance-of-power groups (see propositions 2 and 3), the entailment is that "modern presidents have been particularly sensitive to urban and minority interests—modern presidents of both parties, this is to say, have been more responsive to urban interests than have other factions in their parties."

5. This special consideration by Presidents is perceived as equitable in our pluralistic democracy, because "urban interests in the big states have contended against interests that have a more rural, nativist, and Protestant orientation. The latter interests have tended to dominate Congress, the former the presidency." [Two implicit propositions about the *process* of determining public policy are hidden here. The first is that the Presidency, far more than Congress, is the source of liberal, urban-oriented programs. The second is that the Presidency, with relatively little cooperation from Congress, or even against its active hostility, has effectuated the passage of whatever liberal, urban-oriented programs the nation now has or may have.]

6. One consequence of adopting direct election would be a predicted shift of

electoral influence away from the populous states with their liberal, metropolitan bloc to smaller, conservative states and localities. Black citizens in particular would lose their alleged "special leverage" in presidential politics. The black votes presumed necessary for carrying New York or Michigan would no longer be courted, according to Bickel. "Enough to get millions of votes there, which can be added to the large majorities on the Border, in the South, in Southern California, and in solid Republic country in the middle."[2] Bickel has bought all of Kevin Phillips' argument.[3] [Implicit propositions: that the national electorate is predominantly small town and rural in its demographic characteristics and predominantly conservative (maybe even racist?) in its political orientation.]

Bickel fears that "Direct election would create a presidency with little or no incentive to act as a counterweight to Congress, and as a particular spokesman for urban and minority groups." This portends possible changes in the "ethnic politics of the presidency," diminishing the influence of "blacks, Jews, Irish, Puerto Ricans, and Italians, among others," write Sayre and Parris.

The groups cited by Sayre and Parris as gaining electoral influence are southern whites and blacks (if they voted), and German-, Scandinavian-, and Anglo-Americans in the Midwest.

Six Hypotheses in Search of a Test

The urban interests argument should have an innate appeal to political science. It is potentially more than political rhetoric because (1) all its propositions are statements of empirical behavior, (2) their logical interrelationships give the propositions an important property of a narrow- to middle-range theory, and (3) the propositions are, in principle, capable of being stated in terms of testable hypotheses, i.e., of being invalidated on the basis of empirical evidence.

It is the absence of the third condition that robs the argument of intellectual (or, at least, scientific) respectability. With one exception, dealt with below, the purveyors of the argument offer no evidence to support their propositions. Indeed, they have a tendency to cover their flanks against the possibility of empirical invalidation by using conditional statements and caveats which blunt the impact of contrary empirical evidence. Thus, Bickel's plea to the jury:

The electoral college does *not guarantee* the presidency to a Democrat or to a liberal. The system does require *both parties* to at least *make inroads* in the urban and minority vote *in order to win*. It thus opens up for cohesive groups of liberal orientation in large industrial states a *possibility* of influence that they would *not otherwise have*, even though it holds out *no guarantee* that the influence will *always be effective*.[4] (Emphasis added.)

This is a slippery argument to come to grips with. *Not* because it refuses to "guarantee" a given outcome (political science is resigned to dealing with probability statements rather than universal laws), but because the outcome is not specified in any testable manner. If the Electoral College "does not guarantee" that the President will be a Democrat, a liberal, or both, how often must a Republican, a conservative, or both, be elected before one concludes that the Electoral College has little or no influence as an independent variable? Similarly, how big must be the "inroads" that both parties must make in the urban and minority vote "in order to win?" Was Barry Goldwater's 6 percent of the nonwhite vote in 1964 too small for him to win, but Richard Nixon's 12 percent in 1968 big enough? If so, why didn't Nixon's 32 percent of the nonwhite vote in 1960 carry him to victory? Clearly, other things were not equal.

Finally, while "possibility" statements are attached to urban influence under the Electoral College (with no hint as to how such influence might be measured in terms of public policy outputs), something approaching an absolute statement is made that such influence would be lost under direct election ("... a possibility of influence that they would not otherwise have ... "). It isn't cricket to make conditional statements about the existence of a phenomenon in one institutional setting (the Electoral College) and absolute statements about the absence of the same phenomenon under a different setting (direct election) without supporting evidence for either statement.

What remains to be done, then, is to state the propositions of the urban interests argument in the form of testable hypotheses, to delineate the available empirical evidence and/or future conditions requisite to testing these hypotheses, to set some standard of empirical evidential weight for the tests applied, to apply the tests, and to appraise the validity of the hypotheses in the light of the results of the tests.

The hypotheses are stated below. Closely related hypotheses—those stemming from the same construct or tested with similar kinds of data—are designated by the same Arabic number and different alphabetical letters:

1. In close elections within the most populous states, these states can be "swung" to one candidate or another by a liberal bloc of metropolitan voters.

2. Because this bloc is, by definition, "liberal," we would expect the most populous states to go predominantly (e.g., more than 50 percent of the time) to the most liberal available presidential candidate. We assume such a candidate is always a Democrat. Failing such a Democratic advantage, we may question one or both of the following assumptions: there *is* a cohesive metropolitan bloc; the bloc is liberal.

3. A. Accepted premise: In a nationwide, direct election, the goal of each candidate would be to amass a large, popular vote plurality. In such elections, voters in large states would lose electoral influence to voters in less populous, but politically more homogeneous states, because the more homogeneous states would turn in larger popular vote pluralities than the large states.

3. B. Unaccepted premise: Voters in smaller, more homogeneous states (those which yield high pluralities) are politically more conservative than voters (especially metropolitan voters) in large, heterogeneous states. Therefore (if the premise were valid), taking all homogeneous, high plurality states together, both big states and small, on balance (a) we would expect liberal (Democratic) candidates to net smaller popular vote pluralities than conservative (Republican) candidates in the high plurality states, and (b) we would expect liberal (Democratic) candidates to win nationwide pluralities which are larger than their pluralities in the high plurality states.

4. Blacks, in particular, would lose electoral influence in direct election of the President.

5. Under direct election, public policy positions of the President would become more conservative because liberal bloc voters would be outvoted by conservative voters.

6. Under direct election, national public policy would become more conservative because, in the past, it has been liberal Presidents who have both originated and effectuated liberal programs against a predominantly conservative Congress.

Hypothesis 1: Liberal "Swing" Voters

Empirically, the liberal, swing voter hypothesis is a contradiction in terms. If we operationally define a "swing vote" group as one that does *not* frequently give 51 percent or more of its votes to presidential candidates of the same party, then the liberal, urban groups are not swing voters. Except for selected defections induced by McGovern's candidacy in 1972, such groups consistently give majorities to Democratic candidates.[5]

For the five presidential elections from 1952 through 1968, Democratic voters among nonwhites ranged from 61 percent in 1956 to 94 percent in 1964. Nonwhites also registered an 87 percent vote for McGovern in 1972. From 1952 to 1968, the Democratic vote among Jews ranged from 75 percent in 1956 to 81 percent in 1960, with about 60 percent voting Democratic in 1972. Nationwide data specific to Irish, Italians, and Puerto Ricans are not available. But it is reasonable to assume that these ethnic groups, along with Poles and many Americans whose forebears hail from the Balkan states, are subsumed under Catholics. The percentage of Catholics who voted Democratic ranges from 51 percent in 1956 to 78 percent in 1960, but dipped to 48 percent in 1972. Finally, members of labor union families voted Democratic by percentages ranging from 56 percent in 1968 to 73 percent in 1964, with 46 percent voting for McGovern in 1972.[6]

Hypothesis 2: Tipping the Big States

Even if they admit the swing-vote hypothesis is invalid, proponents of the urban interests argument take shelter behind a fallback position. It is not so much their "swing" characteristic that makes urban minorities important, they contend, but that they are critically situated in the large, competitive states with huge blocs of electoral votes that can be tipped to the presidential candidate of their choice. As demonstrated above, their choice is usually a Democrat. Thus, we can test the second hypothesis that if populous states can be tipped in the direction willed by the urban or metropolitan bloc, most of these states should go Democratic more than 50 percent of the time, i.e., in a proportion greater than chance.

The eleven most populous states (whose combined electoral votes exceeded a majority of the Electoral College in 1972) are listed in Table 3-1.

Table 3-1 shows which party carried each of these states in each of the four presidential elections of the New Deal period and the seven elections in the post-New Deal era. If the metropolitan bloc can be credited with carrying any or

Table 3-1
Partisan Choice of Big Eleven States: 1932-1972 (D = Democratic; R = Republican)

State	Four New Deal Elections					Seven Post-New Deal Elections							
	'32	'36	'40	'44	Number of Democratic Wins Out of Four	'48	'52	'56	'60	'64	'68	'72	Number of Democratic Wins Out of Seven
Calif.	D	D	D	D	4	D	R	R	R	D	R	R	2
Fla.	D	D	D	D	4	D	R	R	R	D	R	R	2
Ill.	D	D	D	D	4	D	R	R	D	D	R	R	3
Ind.	D	D	R	R	2	R	R	R	R	D	R	R	1
Mass.	D	D	D	D	4	D	R	R	D	D	D	D	5
Mich.	D	D	R	D	3	R	R	R	D	D	D	R	3
N.J.	D	D	D	D	4	R	R	R	D	D	R	R	2
N.Y.	D	D	D	D	4	R	R	R	D	D	D	R	3
Ohio	D	D	D	R	3	D	R	R	R	D	R	R	2
Pa.	R	D	D	D	3	R	R	R	D	D	D	R	3
Tex.	D	D	D	D	4	D	R	R	D	D	D	R	4
Number of Democratic states out of eleven	10	11	9	9		6	0	0	7	11	5	1	

all of these states for the Democrats to a degree greater than chance, it was in the New Deal era. Only Indiana, which went Democratic two of four times, failed to exceed the 50 percent criterion. No less than 9 of the 11 states always went Democratic during the heyday of Franklin Roosevelt.

But the elections of the post-New Deal period are a different story. Even if we generously stipulate that three of these seven elections can be considered "half," only Texas and Massachusetts exceeded the 50 percent mark by going Democratic more than three times. And the four states with the largest metropolises, the most potent urban machines, strong unions, and heavy concentrations of blacks and white ethnics—Illinois, Michigan, New York, and Pennsylvania—sent their large blocs of electoral votes into the Democratic column in only three of the post-Roosevelt elections. Collectively, *in close elections when they were most needed*, the big states went Democratic in a proportion greater than chance in 1960 (7 of 11) but less than chance in 1968 (5 of 11). The Democratic disasters of the Eisenhower era and Nixon's re-election in 1972 are self-evident. So is the countervailing *nationwide* Democratic landslide of 1964.

The urban, Democratic voters no longer dominate the presidential politics of their states, largely because they are outnumbered by suburbanites, most of whom tend to cast Republican ballots.[7] There is no cohesive "metropolitan bloc."

This does not, of course, even consider the accretion of Republican votes from the small cities and rural hinterland. When added to the votes of the metropolitan suburbs, these votes can, in the words of Senator Jacob Javits, "cancel out" the votes of the largest cities. For this reason, Javits observes, the attention candidates pay to big states such as New York or California is not necessarily centered on minority groups in the city, but may be just as effectively directed at a strong showing in other areas of the state.

To summarize, the second hypothesis has not been validated.

Paradoxically, two of the academic members of the urban interests school are cognizant of the traps in their reasoning. Sayre and Parris recognize that "any one of a number of voting groups can be identified as crucial," that "suburbs as well as core-city areas" can determine the outcome in a state, that "suburban electorates are growing more rapidly than are central city electorates," and most critically of all, that "there is no assurance that the views of all groups in metropolitan areas will always be liberal or internationalist."

How do they resolve these remarks with their espousal of the urban interests attack on direct election? By the following reasoning: granted that "the predominant views and even the balance of power may shift within the large metropolitan areas; *but in any case* they have important leverage in presidential elections that they would not have without the general-ticket [unit rule] electoral-vote system." (Emphasis added.)

The leverage "in any case" argument can have only two possible interpretations. The first is the traditional concept of an electoral bloc. If this is the correct interpretation, then Sayre and Parris ignore the necessarily *cohesive* property of electoral bloc influence. The error is to assume that an aggregation of voters has "leverage" despite the fact that it splits its vote among two or more parties. To speak of metropolitan areas in bloc terms is a politically meaningless reification when there is no bloc—when inner city majorities go Democratic and suburban and exurban majorities vote Republican. One side's candidate must win, one side's candidate must lose.

The second interpretation sidesteps the pitfalls of the first by maintaining that, *because metropolitan voters can carry states with large electoral votes, both parties nominate candidates that are more liberal than they otherwise would be*. In short, the fact that inner cities may vote for Democrats and suburbs for Republicans is irrelevant if *both* Democratic and Republican candidates lean toward the middle to middle-left, and neither are really "right." The implication is that with a direct election system, one or both parties would nominate more conservative candidates than they do under the status quo. But this implication must be based on the premise or hypothesis that *there are more conservatives in the electorate-at-large than there are liberals*. Since this premise is tested as the fifth hypothesis, its validity will be dealt with below.

However, at this point we can give the hypothesis a rough and ready test. If it were true, then in any election in which a liberal candidate faced a "genuine" conservative, the liberal should have won the election *primarily* because he carried most or all of the Big Eleven states, and we ought to see the conservative candidate (1) winning a goodly number of small and medium-sized states, *or* (2) winning a respectably large share of the nationwide popular vote, *or* (3) both. Two elections of the modern era, 1936 and 1964, can be said to have had a "genuine" conservative opponent for a liberal. In 1936, Alfred M. Landon, running against the New Deal, carried two states, Maine and Vermont. In 1964, Barry Goldwater carried six states, five of them in the deep South, primarily on the basis of his states' rights position. Goldwater received 38.5 percent of the popular vote and Landon won 36.5 percent—both among the all-time lows for major party candidates.

If both parties refrain from nominating outright conservatives these days, it is less because the metropolitan areas utilize the unit rule than because the nation-at-large will not have them. And, recognizing this, both parties have followed historical demands for an accepted degree of the welfare state.

Another Cut: Relative Voting Power of Urban Groups. The preceding discussion helps to place in realistic, political perspective the mathematical-gaming evidence that most urban groups *do* have a form of electoral advantage under the Electoral College. To display and appraise such evidence, we must refer in some detail to the work of Banzhaf and its discussion and extension by Longley and Yunker.[8]

Beginning with the gaming assumption that voting power is the probability of each voter to affect the outcome of an election, Banzhaf's analysis of the Electoral College System followed three stages. He first determined the chance each state has of casting the pivotal tie-breaking vote in creating an Electoral College majority. Banzhaf next determined the number of voting combinations, out of all possible voting combinations of citizen-voters, in which any given citizen-voter can, by *changing his vote*, alter the way his state's electoral votes will be cast. (The term "citizen-voter" is used because Banzhaf's calculations are based on census data, rather than on the number of actual voters, in keeping with the apportionment of electoral votes largely upon population.) In the third stage, the results of the first two steps were combined *to calculate the chance each voter has of affecting the presidential election* through the instrumentality of his state's electoral votes. These chances were normalized by giving the state whose citizens have the least chance of affecting an election (the District of Columbia) a voting power index of one, and setting the voting power indices of all other states at values greater than one. The result is an index of *relative* voting power of the citizen-voter in each state compared to the citizen-voter in every other state.

Based on the index of relative voting power, the citizen-voters of the most highly populated states do, indeed, enjoy a relatively greater chance to determine an election's outcome than the citizen-voters in smaller and medium-sized states. New York and California citizen-voters, for example, have the most opportunity—3.312 and 3.162 chances respectively, compared to 1 chance for District of Columbia voters, who choose only three electors. (There is sufficient population in the nation's capital to entitle it to four electoral votes. It is constrained by the Twenty-third Amendment, which limits the District to no more electoral votes than the number held by the least populous state. It appears that electoral equity for black citizens in the District is correlated with the birth rate of Eskimos in Alaska.) Similarly, the only other states with an index of relative voting power of 2 or above are New Jersey, Michigan, Texas, Ohio, Illinois, and Pennsylvania. With direct election, all voters in all states would have the same index of voting power—1.

Longley and Yunker build upon Banzhaf's work in several imaginative ways. The one most germane to our purpose is their calculations of relative voting power for various groups, differing in the size of their place of residence, ethnic and occupational characteristics, and region of the country. The first step is to calculate a *national average* index of per-citizen voting power. The number of citizen-voters in a state (the state's population) is multiplied by Banzhaf's index of relative voting power for citizens in that state. These 51 products (including the District of Columbia) are summed, then the sum is divided by the total number of citizen-voters in the nation (the total population). The resulting quotient is the national average per-citizen voting power. It is 2.158. This index can then be compared to the average voting power of various groups. The second step is computing such group averages. For example, the average voting power of all urban residents under the Electoral College is calculated by multiplying each state's relative voting power index (from Banzhaf) by its number of urban residents. The sum of these 51 products, divided by the total number of urban residents in the nation, equals the national average voting power per urban resident. The third step is to calculate the percent deviation of this urban average from the previously determined national average of per-citizen voting power, which is 2.158. The same process is followed in calculating percent deviations from the national per-citizen average for the other groups considered. "This percent deviation gives an indication of how this particular group in the electorate fares in comparison with other groups, as well as with all of the electorate."

Since the national per-citizen average does not deviate from itself, its percent deviation value is zero. All other groups are then scaled against this zero value, with plus signs if their percent deviation is above the per-citizen average and minus signs if their percent deviation is below the average. Longley and Yunker's findings are arrayed in Table 3-2.

On the basis of the measurement used, the urban interests argument appears to be supported. Residents of central cities are advantaged, but not quite as much as residents of their suburbs. Residents of both coastal areas have an advantage over citizens of the South and Middle America. The pro-Democratic blue collar workers are slightly ahead of the average citizen, and traditionally

Table 3-2
Percentage Deviations from National Average Voting Power for Selected Groups Under the Electoral College

Residency Groups		Ethnic and Occupation Groups		Regional Groups	
Suburbs[a]	+9.1%	Foreign stock	+10.2%	Far West	+26.5%
Central cities	+8.0	Blue collar	+2.5	East	+14.2
SMSA's	+7.2	National average	0.0	National average	0.0
Urban areas	+4.2	Blacks	−5.1	Midwest	−4.2
National average	0.0			South	−15.4
Rural nonfarm	−8.0			Mountain states	−38.4
Rural	−9.6				
Rural farm	−14.6				

[a]Defined as urban areas other than central cities within SMSA's.
Source: Adapted from Lawrence Longley and John Yunker, "Who Is Really Advantaged By the Electoral College–And Who Just Thinks He Is?," a paper presented at the 67th Annual Meeting of the American Political Science Association, Chicago, Ill., September 7-11, 1971, figures 10, 11, and 12. The same data also appear in Lawrence Longley and Alan Braun, THE POLITICS OF ELECTORAL COLLEGE REFORM (New Haven: Yale University Press, 1972), 123.

Democratic first- and second-generation ethnics of foreign stock have a considerable advantage. But black citizens have markedly less opportunity to influence elections than does the average citizen-voter. As Longley and Yunker note, this is because of high concentrations of the black population in medium-sized states of the deep South, such as Alabama, Georgia, Louisiana, and Mississippi. This point will be developed below.

However, the foregoing is literally a numbers game. For this reason, it is also a "numbers game" in the rhetorical sense that the findings have little relevance to the real world of presidential elections. This is demonstrated by Longley and Yunker, who exhibit intellectual rectitude in their discussion of the limitations embodied in their analysis. Distilled and somewhat amended, these limitations are as follows:

First, Banzhaf's indices of relative voting power are a theoretical measure of a citizen's long-range, average chance of affecting the outcome of an election. Although they reflect inequalities built into the electoral structure, they do not consider such other crucial political variables as one-party domination in a state and voter turnout. Both may affect a citizen's voting power in any given election.

Second, the Banzhaf indices are based on relative, not absolute, probabilities of affecting an election outcome. As such, the indices are likely to overestimate the value of the pivotal power approach in large electorates. Although pivotal power may be influential in small bodies, e.g., courts and legislative committees, it is dissipated in an electorate of upwards of 70 million.

In absolute terms, the chance a citizen in state A has of changing the outcome of the election is very small in comparison with the chance that a Supreme Court Justice has of changing the outcome of a case. Hence, the *relative* power differences, though they are evident in the present Electoral College and proposed systems other than the direct vote plan, may be severely outweighed by the extremely low *absolute* chances of a citizen affecting the outcome.[9]

The third and fourth limitations inhere in the crucial assumptions made in the pivotal power, or tie-breaking vote, concept itself. The central assumption is that the only meaningful vote is the one that breaks a tie. This, in turn, means that the *sole object* of the game is to *win by casting the tie-breaking vote*. But as Mann and Shapley observe about their own pivotal power study based on 51 states, "[W]e are forced to insist that the players (i.e., the states) all be independent agents, free from prior commitments and uninfluenced by considerations outside the stated objectives of the game. These unrealistic assumptions would at once invalidate any attempt to apply the power indices in an actual presidential campaign."[10] The same constraints would apply to individual citizen-voters in Banzhaf's analysis, for the voter's objective is not to become pivotal by, for example, changing his intended vote to alter the outcome. It is to vote for the candidate to whom he is already committed, for whatever reasons of issue-, party-, or personality-orientation that are sufficient unto the voter. Moreover, even if the voter did consider his sole objective as affecting the outcome, there is no way of his knowing before the election if, and in what combination with others, he could be pivotal. Thus, because of imperfect information, as well as prior political commitment, the voter cannot act as an independent agent.

The fourth limitation is that because the pivotal power concept assigns power only to the single, tie-breaking vote, additional votes inflating the size of the majority are not considered powerful under the rules of the game. But in practical presidential politics, the size of the winner's majority can be exceedingly important. Presidents who win by landslides tend to have longer, and far more romantic, honeymoons with Congress than Presidents who barely win. This is especially true if fellow partisans ride in on his coattails to swell the President's support on the Hill.[11] To the extent that the electorate casts its vote for a President not as an end, but as a means of affecting public policy, it is in their interest, too, to accrue as many votes as possible beyond the pivotal one.

Finally, the voting power analysis skirts the problems of demonstrating voters' influence over a candidate's issue positions and excluding voters outside the winning coalition from receiving some rewards.

We agree with Longley and Yunker that Banzhaf's analysis (and their own extension of it), being "divorced from the political realities of party affiliation and voting, does not at all examine the coalitions of voters which have formed in actual presidential elections."

It is to this task, begun with the testing of hypotheses 1 and 2, that we now return in considering hypotheses 3.A and 3.B.

Hypotheses 3.A and B:
Who Wins the Big Pluralities?

Sayre and Parris contend that under direct election,

The electoral power of each state would no longer depend on the size of its total electoral vote bloc but instead on the size of the popular vote margin the state gave the winning candidate. The plan would place a premium on areas where a candidate could roll up large popular pluralities. This would mean prominence for a different group of states than the eleven with the most electoral votes under the existing system.

The last sentence is the basis for hypothesis 3.A, *that the Big Eleven states will turn in smaller total pluralities than other states and, consequently, lose electoral influence to the smaller states.* Sayre and Parris offer what they consider empirical support for the hypothesis by listing the states which had turned in popular vote pluralities of at least 100,000 votes in the close presidential elections of 1960 and 1968. These states, with Big Eleven states indicated by italics, are as follows:

1960 (12 states): Georgia, *Indiana*, Iowa, Kansas, Louisiana, *Massachusetts*, Nebraska, *New York*, *Ohio*, Oklahoma, *Pennsylvania*, Rhode Island.

1968 (21 states): Alabama, *California, Florida*, Georgia, *Illinois, Indiana*, Iowa, Kansas, Louisiana, *Massachusetts, Michigan*, Minnesota, Mississippi, Nebraska, *New York*, North Carolina, Oklahoma, *Pennsylvania*, Rhode Island, Virginia, District of Columbia (considered a "state" for present purposes).

From the above list, Sayre and Parris conclude: "Thus the direct-vote plan would mean a strategic position for the states that are politically more homogeneous as well as at least fairly populous," and "Smaller cities, towns, and rural areas would gain relative to metropolitan areas."

These conclusions outrun the data base in a number of ways. To dispose of two lesser problems, their two lists constitute an intersection of the sets of Big Eleven states and other states. To this extent, the magnitude of relative loss of Big Eleven state "electoral power" to "a different group of states" is problematic. Secondly, the discussion suddenly shifts from states as jurisdictions to "smaller cities, towns, and rural areas," with no methodological gearing down for this transition.

More importantly, utilizing a single, open-ended category of a 100,000 vote plurality or more hides a wealth of variation in the size of these pluralities from state to state. The pluralities range from 110,530 in Rhode Island in 1960 to 510,424 in Massachusetts in the same year. Also, the listing says nothing about the *distribution of these pluralities among different presidential candidates*. It is idle to talk about one *group* of states being more homogeneous than another group if, in fact, within the *same* group one state's Republican plurality is offset by another state's Democratic plurality.

Most critically of all, the Big Eleven states with large pluralities would lose "electoral power" *only* if their *net pluralities* for *one* candidate were exceeded by *net pluralities* for *another* candidate in other high plurality states. Finally, since Presidents are elected by the entire nation, not by selected groups of states, high plurality, Big Eleven states would lose "voting power" in a direct election *only* if the *net pluralities* for their candidate among *all* high plurality states were lower than the nationwide popular vote plurality for their candidate.

These considerations constitute the theoretical rationale for hypothesis 3.B. Assuming that Democratic candidates win net pluralities in the Big Eleven states (an assumption validated below), hypothesis 3.B states that (a) liberal (Democratic) candidates will net smaller popular vote pluralities than conservative (Republican) candidates in the high plurality states, and (b) liberal (Democratic) candidates would win national pluralities that are larger than the Democratic net pluralities in the high plurality states.

Both hypotheses, 3.A and 3.B, are tested by the data arrayed in Table 3-3. These data are from the high plurality states of 1960 and 1968 as defined by Sayre and Parris (pluralities of 100,000 votes or more).

As can be observed from comparing the total pluralities of Big Eleven states

Table 3-3

States with Popular Vote Pluralities of at Least 100,000: 1960 and 1968 (in thousands of votes)

		Election of 1960				
	Number of	Plurality		Electoral Votes		
Candidate	States	Number	%	Number	%	
Five States of Big Eleven						
Kennedy	3	1,010	67	93	71	
Nixon	2	496	33	38	29	
Total	5	1,506	100	131	100	
Seven Other States						
Kennedy	3	471	41	26	45	
Nixon	4	681	59	32	55	
Total	7	1,152	100	58	100	

Exhibit:

Popular Vote Pluralities
For the 12 big plurality states, a Democratic plurality of 304,000
For the nation, a Democratic plurality of 113,000

Electoral Vote Pluralities
For the 12 big plurality states, a Democratic net plurality of 49
For the nation, a Democratic plurality of 84

		Election of 1968				
	Number of	Plurality		Electoral Votes		
Candidate	States	Number	%	Number	%	
Eight States of Big Eleven						
Nixon	4	830	36	93	46	
Humphrey	4	1,465	64	107	54	
Wallace	–	–	–	–	–	
Total	8	2,295	100	200	100	
Thirteen Other States						
Nixon	6	895	36	54	49	
Humphrey	3	432	18	17	16	
Wallace	4	1,136	46	39	35	
Total	13	2,463	100	110	100	

Exhibit:

Popular Vote Pluralities
For the 21 big plurality states, a *Democratic* plurality of 172,000
For the nation, a *Republican* plurality of 510,000

Electoral Vote Pluralities
For the 21 big plurality states, a Republican plurality of 23
For the nation, a Republican plurality of 110

Source: Popular vote pluralities and electoral votes won from POLITICS IN AMERICA, 3rd ed. (Washington, D.C.: Congressional Quarterly Service, May 1969), 125 and 127. Percentages computed by author.

to other states, hypothesis 3.A is invalid for the election of 1960 but valid for the 1968 election. In the whisker-close 1960 election, the total plurality from the five Big Eleven states exceeded that of the seven other high plurality states by 354,000 votes, 1,506,000 to 1,152,000. The direction, but not the magnitude, was reversed in 1968, when the total plurality for 13 other states was but 168,000 votes greater than the total for eight Big Eleven states, 2,463,000 to 2,295,000. Considering that 1960 was a much closer election than 1968 (Kennedy's national plurality was 113,000 in 1960, Nixon's was 510,000 in 1968), one is not impressed by the argument that in close national elections Big Eleven states will lose voting power to other states.

But more importantly, *neither group of states was homogeneous in either election*. Both groups split up among at least two candidates. This split is evident using several different measures—the number of states within each group that is carried by each candidate, the size of the plurality carried by each candidate (both in absolute and percentage terms), and the electoral votes won by each candidate (both in absolute and percentage terms). In partisan terms, democratic candidates were favored among Big Eleven states. Democrats won handsome majorities of both popular votes and electoral votes in both elections. Conversely, the Republican candidate bettered the Democrat in the seven other states in 1960, while in 1968 the Republican ran second to George Wallace in popular votes but won the most electoral votes in 13 other states.

In short, there are not simply "homogeneous" states; there are Democratic states and Republican states. And now, probably, there are, or may be, Wallace states. This is nothing new. The partisan direction of pluralities will be of importance in a direct election system up to, but no more than, the same extent it is under the Electoral College system—in determining who will win the election.

That brings us to hypothesis 3.B. As shown in the exhibits of "Popular Vote Pluralities" in Table 3-3, both parts of hypothesis 3.B are invalidated for both elections. Among all the high plurality states, the Democratic candidate won a larger net popular vote plurality than the Republican candidate, not a smaller one. And in nationwide terms, in both elections the Democratic candidate *won more popular votes from all the high plurality states than he won in the nation as a whole, not less*. Kennedy's 1960 plurality over Nixon in high plurality states was almost three times the size of his nationwide plurality. *In 1968, Humphrey beat Nixon by 172,000 votes in the high plurality states while Nixon won the nation with a 510,000-vote plurality over Humphrey*.

Democratic candidates also seem to do better in winning popular votes than electoral votes in the high plurality states. As demonstrated in the exhibits of "Electoral Vote Pluralities," in 1960 Kennedy won 49 more electoral votes than Nixon in the high plurality states, compared to 84 more electoral votes than Nixon in the entire country. Yet Kennedy's popular vote margin over Nixon in the high plurality states was, to repeat, three times his national popular plurality.

The 1968 election presents a similar pattern. Among the high plurality states, Humphrey received 172,000 more popular votes than Nixon, but Nixon won 23 more electoral votes than Humphrey. If the 1960 and 1968 elections are any guide (and they were selected by Sayre and Parris to buttress *their* case, not ours), Democrats would fare better in the high plurality states under direct election than they would with the Electoral College.

What does it all mean?

1. It means that the conventional wisdom that the most populous states are highly competitive compared to other states is a myth. Although the Republican-Democratic split of the popular vote in these states may be relatively close in *percentage terms*, when translated into the absolute numbers of popular votes cast, there are huge popular vote pluralities to be won in each state, and in the Big Eleven states collectively. This is largely because these states contain a vast reservoir of voters.

2. It means that because politicians "go where the ducks are," candidates of both parties will continue to pay attention to, and actively campaign in, the most populous states and their large metropolitan centers, under a system of direct election. Experienced campaign managers of both political parties *have already so stated.*[12]

3. It means that even in close elections the popular vote pluralities of the Big Eleven states tend to split favorably for Democratic candidates with a clear urban and liberal bias (Kennedy and Humphrey as cases in point). Consequently, there is no reason to believe that the cities will lose whatever influence they may have had over Democratic presidential politics, or whatever lesser influence they may have had in liberalizing Republican presidential politics.

Hypothesis 4: What's In It for the Blacks?

Invalidation of the preceding hypotheses impugns the credibility of the hypothesis that black voters would lose influence under direct election. That hypothesis can be completely laid to rest if the likelihood of two propositions can be demonstrated:

1. Blacks could effectively transfer their voting strength, actual and potential, to the national stage and be considerably effective there. "The newly enfranchised blacks from southern states like Georgia and Alabama would be able to combine their votes with blacks from New York, Illinois, and Michigan and thus constitute a formidable national voting bloc that the parties would ignore at their peril."

2. A necessary, if not sufficient, condition for the first proposition is that discriminatory practices intended to keep southern blacks from the polls are eliminated.

Evidence supporting the first proposition is arrayed in Table 3-4, which shows the incidence of voting participation of blacks by region and place of residence in 1968. The total number of blacks who voted in the South, nearly 3.1 million, almost equals the 3.2 million who went to the polls in the North and West. But under the unit rule of the Electoral College, the three million black votes in the South were translated into electoral votes for Richard Nixon or George Wallace in all the states but Texas.

However, it is the sizable number of *potential* black votes in the South that should give direct election a special appeal to liberals. The number of blacks who did not vote totaled nearly 2.9 million in the South compared to 1.7 million in the North and West. The nonvoting black citizens in the South reside in about equal numbers in SMSAs and nonmetropolitan areas. In the North, the lion's share of nonvoting blacks (1.3 million out of 1.7 million) reside in the large metropolitan areas with populations in excess of one million. (See Exhibit in Table 3-4.)

Table 3-4
Blacks of Voting Age—Voting Participation by Region and Size of Place of Residence: November 1968 (numbers in thousands; percentages in parentheses)

Residence	North and West			South		
	Total	Voted	Did Not Vote	Total	Voted	Did Not Vote
Metropolitan (SMSAs)[a]	4,651 (100.0)	3,033 (65.2)	1,619 (34.8)	3,158 (100.0)	1,720 (54.5)	1,438 (45.5)
Non-Metro[b]	293 (100.0)	173 (59.2)	119 (40.8)	2,832 (100.0)	1,374 (48.5)	1,459 (51.5)
Total, all Blacks	4,944 (100.0)	3,206 (64.8)	1,738 (23.8)	5,991 (100.0)	3,094 (51.6)	2,898 (48.4)
Exhibit: Large Metro (SMSAs of 1 million or more)	3,680 (100.0)	2,419 (65.7)	1,261 (34.3)	1,166 (100.0)	608 (52.2)	558 (47.8)

[a]For definitional characteristics of SMSAs, see p. 5 of source cited below, or any Bureau of the Census publication utilizing SMSAs.

[b]All population not living in SMSAs, composed of nonfarm (non-SMSA urban areas and rural persons not on farms) and farm population. For more detailed definitional characteristics, see p. 6 of source cited below, or any Bureau of the Census publication utilizing these concepts.

Source: U.S. Bureau of the Census, CURRENT POPULATION REPORTS, Series P-20, No. 192, "Voting and Registration in the Election of November 1968," (Washington, D.C.: U.S. Government Printing Office, 1969), Tables 2 and 3, pp. 13-17.

The pattern is clear. Two large, untapped reservoirs of black voters lie in the major cities of the North and West and, especially, in the urban and rural South. The three channels needed to unite these bodies are direct election, vigorous enforcement of civil rights statutes guaranteeing the right to register and vote, and active registration and get-out-the-vote campaigns by political organizations.

That brings us to the conditional proposition—the extent to which discriminatory practices, especially in the South, can be diminished or eliminated. Certainly the public record, both legal and political, tends to support the proposition that the incidence of voting discrimination has waned, and would continue to diminish, under direct election. Consider these items:

1. In 1970 Congress extended the duration of the Voting Rights Act of 1965 to 1975. The act suspends literacy tests in selected southern states and provides for the registration of southern blacks by federal registrars. These provisions of the 1965 act, and the states covered by them, continue under the 1970 extension. An amendment adopted in 1970 suspended literacy tests for all elections in all states until 1975.[13]

2. In August 1972, the Gallup poll reported:

For the first time in polling history, as high a proportion of non-whites as whites say they are registered [to vote]. While the national figure for all adults has increased only four points since the study earlier this year—from 71 percent to 75 percent—the figure for non-whites nationwide has increased 8 percentage points—from 66 percent to 74 percent. The most dramatic increase in registration is recorded among non-whites in the South.[14]

3. The likelihood is great that the increase in blacks registering would be buttressed by practical political considerations. When interviewed by Peirce a few years ago, experienced political campaign managers of both parties "agreed that a direct vote would also increase the pressure to register the greatest pool of voters who do not yet participate fully in U.S. presidential elections—the blacks of the South. They also anticipated an effort to reach the 'missing million' of black males (mostly in northern cities) who have never been registered, and to register the migrating citizen and get him to the polls."

Hypothesis 5: Are Most Americans Conservative?

The fifth hypothesis contends that under direct election, a President would be more conservative on civil rights and social welfare issues *because* such policy postures would reflect the majority sentiment of the American electorate at large. The hypothesis is inferred from assumptions about the conservatism of old-line American, white Anglo-Saxon Protestants living in the South and in the small cities and rural areas of Middle America.

Besides positing a more direct linkage between public opinion and public policy than necessarily exists,[15] the hypothesis is not supported by knowledge about the direction and structure of public opinion gained from many academic and commercial opinion polls. Indeed, the findings of such polls constitute evidence invalidating the hypothesis.

Before examining this evidence, we must first distinguish between civil rights and "law and order." The former refers to such legislative and judicial policies as desegregating schools and removing discrimination in job opportunities, voting rights, and access to public accommodations. The latter reflects opposition to violent demonstrations (or demonstrations that become involved in violence) and especially opposition to street crimes and to urban riots, with their attendant looting, fire bombing, and sniping. In the course of his interviews with the public in 1968, Lubell found strong negative attitudes toward the "excesses" tied into the law and order issue. But when respondents were asked which civil rights laws enacted in the past 15 years they would keep or repeal, "The overwhelming majority expressed no desire to turn back the civil rights clock."[16] Two exceptions were open housing laws and school busing (an *instrument* of overt integration), which were opposed by sizable majorities in both North and South.

Similarly, in February 1969 the Harris Poll found that favorable dispositions toward law enforcement were held along with favorable attitudes toward federal aid to education, antipoverty programs, and Medicaid without engendering cognitive or affective dissonance.

Such generalized, nationwide findings can be corroborated by academic research which offers more detail on the incidence of opinion on social welfare issues by region, size of place of residence, and ethnic group. We can test the fifth hypothesis, therefore, not only by asking if a majority of the nation takes essentially conservative positions on social welfare programs, but also if majorities of small city residents, farmers, Protestants, and Americans of English, German, and Scandinavian extraction are conservative. As we shall see, quite the contrary is the case. *Majorities of the nation, and of selected subsample groupings, are liberal in terms of social welfare programs.*

The preceding generalization summarizes the opinion elicited in a 1964 study by Lloyd Free and Hadley Cantril.[17] Their survey was conducted by the Gallup polling organization, and consisted of two samples of about 1,600 respondents each. The first sample was interviewed in late September and early October, the second in the last half of October. Since several items were included in both surveys, there was a combined sample of about 3,200 respondents, which is large enough to permit subsample comparisons among different population groups.

The Free and Cantril study confirms what students of public opinion have long suspected—that Americans tend to respond in a conservative direction to abstract principles that underlie contemporary conservative rhetoric, but simultaneously favor social welfare programs that are the foundation of liberal public policy. Free and Cantril utilize what they term Ideological and Operational

Spectrums in public opinion. These are, respectively, scales based on responses to five items measuring abstract, ideological principles, and five quite different items measuring response to specific social welfare programs. Because the distinction between ideological conservatism and operational (public policy) liberalism is critical, and because we shall emphasize the distribution of group opinion along the Operational Spectrum, the items for both spectrums and the distribution of national public opinion on each of them are presented below. The sample size for each set of five items is given in parenthesis.

Ideological Spectrum ($N = 1,611$):

1. "The federal government is interfering too much in state and local matters." Agree, 40 percent; Disagree, 47 percent; Don't know, 13 percent.

2. "Social problems here in this country could be solved more effectively if the government would only keep its hands off and let people in local communities handle their own problems in their own ways." Agree, 49 percent; Disagree, 38 percent; Don't know, 13 percent.

3. "The government has gone too far in regulating business and interfering with the free enterprise system." Agree, 42 percent; Disagree, 39 percent; Don't know, 19 percent.

4. "Generally speaking, any able-bodied person who really wants to work in this country can find a job and earn a living." Agree, 76 percent; Disagree, 21 percent; Don't know, 3 percent.

5. "We should rely more on individual initiative and not so much on governmental welfare programs." Agree, 79 percent; Disagree, 12 percent; Don't know, 9 percent.

Items 4 and 5 are interesting not only because they are the only ones in which a majority takes a conservative position, but because this position is agreed to by elements in the population whose low income and high incidence of unemployment should, rationally, prompt them to disagree with the statements. Yet seven out of ten respondents with family incomes of less than $5,000 a year agreed that an able-bodied person seeking employment can find it, as did six out of every ten black respondents. Similarly, seven out of ten low income respondents and six out of ten black respondents agreed with the statement that we should rely more on individual initiative than on welfare programs. The Puritan Ethic is as alive and well in the ghetto as in the board room.

But the Social Gospel is a closer interpretation of the overwhelming public support for government programs which insulate the individual from the chilling realities of competition in the "free market place." Free and Cantril found that 75 percent of their respondents agreed that the government has a responsibility to try to reduce unemployment. They also cite Gallup and Harris polls from early 1967 which show that 54 percent of those interviewed favored present or increased levels of spending for the controversial Community Action Program to combat poverty in cities and neighborhoods, 67 percent favored present or increased expenditure levels for the Head Start Program, and 75 percent agreed that retraining poorly educated people for the job market deserved present or increased levels of funding. This liberal perspective is reflected and amplified in the response to items in the Operational Spectrum.

Operational Spectrum (N = 3,215):

1. "A broad general program of federal aid to education is under consideration, which would include federal grants to help pay teachers' salaries. Would you be for or against such a program?" For, 62 percent; Against, 28 percent; Don't know, 10 percent.

2. "Congress has been considering a compulsory medical insurance program covering hospital and nursing home care for the elderly. This Medicare program would be financed out of increased social security taxes. In general, do you approve or disapprove of this program?" Approve, 63 percent; Disapprove, 30 percent; Don't know, 7 percent.

3. "Under the federal housing program, the federal government is making grants to help build low-rent public housing. Do you think government spending for this purpose should be kept at least at the present level, or reduced, or ended altogether?" At least at present level, 63 percent; Reduced, 12 percent; Ended, 10 percent; Don't know, 15 percent.

4. "Under the urban renewal program, the federal government is making grants to help rebuild run-down sections of our cities. Do you think government spending for this purpose should be kept at least at the present level, or reduced, or ended altogether?" At least at present level, 67 percent; Reduced, 10 percent; Ended, 11 percent; Don't know, 12 percent.

5. "The federal government has a responsibility to try to do away with poverty in this country." Agree, 72 percent; Disagree, 20 percent; Don't know, 8 percent.

The distribution of the national sample along both spectrums is presented in Table 3-5, a clear demonstration that the public would not have the government practice what some of its conservative officials preach, even though half the public might agree with the sermon.[18]

The weight of public opinion at the liberal end of the Operational Spectrum remains when opinion is controlled for selected socioeconomic, regional, and political characteristics. As shown in the third column of Table 3-6, a majority of all the selected subsample groups score in the liberal categories. *These majorities are uniform among all the groups which, according to the fifth hypothesis, would combine to form a conservative influence in direct presidential elections—farmers, Protestants, residents of small cities and rural areas, southerners, and white, Anglo-Saxon, old-line Americans of English, German, and Scandinavian extraction.* Even those respondents from southern states which

Table 3-5
Ideological and Operational Spectrums

National Sample	Ideological Spectrum		Operational Spectrum	
Completely liberal	4%	} 16%	44%	} 65%
Predominantly liberal	12		21	
Middle of the road	34	} 34%	21	} 21%
Predominantly conservative	20	} 50%	7	} 14%
Completely conservative	30		7	
Total	100%		100%	
	N = 1,491		N = 3,041	

Source: Lloyd Free and Hadley Cantril, THE POLITICAL BELIEFS OF AMERICANS (New York: Simon and Schuster, 1968), 32, 207, 209.

were carried by Goldwater in 1964 were predominantly liberal, if not in such large proportions as southerners from states carried by Johnson.

Hypothesis 6: President or
Congress? Chicken or Egg?

The sixth hypothesis perceives the public policy process as a kind of political seesaw, with the President sitting at the liberal, activist end and Congress perched on the conservative, passive end. Elect a President by direct vote, the sixth hypothesis warns, and you upset the delicate balance by having the President slide down the board to join Congress at the conservative end.

Even if the balancing image were a valid representation of reality, it has already been demonstrated that direct election *per se* would be unlikely to cause an exchange of liberal, activist Presidents for conservative, ministerial ones. In the presence of the evidence that all segments of the electorate are operationally liberal, the electorate may be expected to elect broadly the same types of President in the future as it did in the past, regardless of whether the electoral system tinkers with popular votes or simply counts them. By failing to validate the fifth hypothesis, we have also failed to validate the sixth. Therefore, *if* Congress is conservative and merely reacts to presidential initiatives, and *if* the President is the only truly liberal, innovating actor of the two, then direct election should not alter these characteristics.

The temptation to leave the sixth hypothesis is strong. But it will be resisted, for there is a growing body of scholarly opinion which contends, with some degree of persuasiveness, that the aforementioned images of the President and Congress are caricatures of reality. This is a many-faceted subject. We will confine our remarks to a bare surface examination of the contentions that the

Table 3-6
Distribution Along Operational Spectrum by Selected Groups

Groups	Completely Liberal	Predominantly Liberal	(Total Liberal)	Middle of Road	Predominantly Conservative	Completely Conservative	Total
National sample (N = 3,041)	44%	21%	(65%)	21%	7%	7%	100%
Farmers[a]	34	24	(58)	21	12	9	100
Protestants[b]	38	22	(60)	22	9	9	100
City Size							
500,000+	55	19	(74)	17	4	5	100
50,000 to 499,999	43	21	(64)	22	8	6	100
2,500 to 49,999	31	24	(55)	25	10	10	100
Under 2,500 and rural	36	23	(59)	23	10	8	100
Region							
East	54	18	(72)	19	5	4	100
South–Goldwater	33	24	(57)	16	10	17	100
South–Johnson	44	23	(67)	18	8	7	100
Midwest	39	23	(62)	23	9	6	100
West	37	22	(59)	25	7	9	100

Ethnic Group						
English[c]	30	21	(51)	27	12	10	100
German[c]	34	20	(54)	28	10	8	100
Scandinavian[c]	39	20	(59)	24	10	7	100

[a]Smallest "total liberal" majority of all occupations, excepting "Professional, business," at 54 percent.

[b]Smallest "completely" or "total liberal" percentages of three major regions.

[c]Smaller "completely" or "total liberal" percentages than Irish Catholics, Italians, and Eastern or Central Europeans.

Source: Same as for Table 3-5, pp. 215-217.

President is the *dominant influence* in the legislative process, that he is the source of *liberal* or innovative proposals (or both), and that he represents the *national* interest against the particularistic or "parochial" interests represented in Congress.

On the question of dominant influence in the legislative process, Chamberlain's 1946 study of 90 major laws enacted in the preceding 50 years found that about 20 percent of them could be credited to the President, roughly 40 percent were the product of Congress, 30 percent were influenced about equally by both branches, and something under 10 percent were pushed through by external pressure groups.[19]

More recent scholarship arrives at essentially the same conclusions about the executive-legislative relationship, in spite of such phenomena as the Republican-southern Democrat Conservative Coalition and a good deal of fashionable talk about presidential and congressional wings in both parties. Cronin examines various case studies of the legislative history of New Frontier and Great Society programs, then concludes that presidential initiatives were tempered and buttressed by Democratic party orientations, the unfinished business of previous Presidents, and by congressional *incubation* of liberal measures and congressional-presidential *dialogue* over their substance.[20]

The spectacular legislative record of the 89th Congress is the case in point. Most of President Johnson's legislative program had been previously "incubated"—kept alive to pick up support, wait a better political climate, or be hatched when the problems it addressed became more important—in Congress. To this must be added the critical variable of the 89th Congress having sufficient northern Democratic *votes* to do for Johnson's program what the 88th Congress was unable to do for most of Kennedy's—pass it.[21]

Similarly, Congress is not a passive recipient of presidential proposals. Nor does it invariably play the parochial, self-interested Roman Senate to the President's noble, disinterested Caesar. As Cronin observes:

Sometimes the presidency, and sometimes Congress, play the dominating role in initiating legislation. But the initiation as well as the enactment of virtually all major legislation in domestic and economic policy matters results from extensive "conversations" between presidency and Congress, and between both of these institutions and strategic interest groups. To conceive of the presidency as representing the *national interest or general welfare* and Congress merely as the tool of *special* or *particularistic interests* is as naive today as it was thirty years ago when Pendleton Herring cautioned—"In fact presidential policy, however 'pure' in motivation, must mean the promotion of certain interests at the expense of others."

The point of all this is not that the President has been downgraded in importance, but that Congress is more important than it has been given credit for. Influence in the legislative process is not a zero-sum game, where one player acquires more only if the other player retains less. To return to our original simile, the legislative process is not "like a seesaw where as one end goes down the other must automatically go up. It is, rather, like a gasoline engine which operates most efficiently when all of its cylinders are functioning."

What the presidential liberals reply, of course, is that the congressional cylinders misfire because they are conservative and ill-represent the popular will. To the extent the charges have validity in terms of past congressional performance, one rejoinder might be that the reapportionment decisions should effect more equitable representation of popular views in the House. There is, of course, no assurance that such views will be liberal enough to please the critics. Most new and reapportioned congressional districts have followed the population to the suburbs. Even allowing for the time lag imposed by the seniority system, the power centers of the House should have a different geographical base a decade or two hence from what they had a decade or two in the past.

However, the reapportionment decisions have not convinced all opponents of direct election that the historical leverage of rural, conservative groups in Congress has been redressed. Bickel, for example, makes a five-point argument. We can present, and deal with it, forthwith:[22]

1. Reapportionment does not affect equal representation of states in the Senate or the constitutional minimum of one House seat for each state, regardless of population.

This is a time-honored ploy in political argumentation—refuse to accept incremental reforms which are possible in lieu of massive renovations which are not. Second, and politically most important, the argument conveniently ignores the fact that liberalism and a social-welfare orientation are not one-to-one correlates with the size or urbanization of the state a Senator represents. One need only call to mind such liberal senators as Mike Mansfield (Montana), Frank Church (Idaho), George McGovern (South Dakota), Harold Hughes (Iowa), Fred Harris (Oklahoma), and Gale McGee (Wyoming). Conversely, large, metropolitan states have sent to the Senate such conservatives as Frank Lausche (Ohio) and Everett Dirksen (Illinois).

2. It would be "foolhardy [writes Bickel] to bank on the permanence of the reapportionment decisions, *just exactly as we now know them*. They are subject to relitigation every decade, with every census." (Emphasis added.)

This is the wispiest of straw men. No champion (or enemy) of direct election assumes that today's legislative district boundary lines will remain unchanged. Indeed, it is opposition to the permanence of district lines despite population shifts that underlies the one man, one vote decisions.

3. Gerrymandering, which the courts have not attempted to control, can accomplish all that malapportionment ever achieved. This is especially the case when the courts throw out other considerations, such as groupings of political subdivisions, in the interests of an overriding criterion of exact mathematical equality.

It is difficult to disequate gerrymandering and malapportionment without a more precise list of their common evils. Bickel's only expressed concern is that political subdivisions (whose residents presumably have common demands with respect to public policy) will be split into different legislative districts for state and/or federal representation. This is a complex issue, not easily resolved in a few sentences. But one can point out that in any kind of tradeoff between having one's township or county remain intact within the boundaries of a single legislative district, or being grossly underrepresented in the legislature because of the massive population of one's district compared to other districts, a citizen might be foolhardy to opt for the former instead of the latter.

4. Bickel suggests that Congress may not be what it is because of malapportionment, but because of its internal methods of distributing power. Notable among these are seniority and the committee system, and the rules of debate, which maximize the possibilities of group veto and minority resistance. Seniority is won by legislators from homogeneous districts with simple concerns, writes Bickel. Such men concentrate single-mindedly in an area of specialization, achieve legislative power in it, and use this power to bargain with their less influential peers. Because legislators from big states and urban districts represent more complex constituencies, they are disadvantaged in the race for seniority and power.

This is a familiar rendering. It combines elements of what Wolfinger and Heifetz call the "textbook theory" and the "insiders' theory."[23] According to the textbook theory, the congressional Democratic party is fragmented because the lack of party competition in the South results in greater seniority for southern Democrats than for northern Democrats. The insiders theory observes that there are many safe seats in the North, especially in big city House districts. But Democrats from these districts fritter away their potential seniority by committee hopping and by leaving the House when an executive or judicial position opens up in their home state.

By empirical investigation, Wolfinger and Heifetz invalidate the "insiders' theory" on every count. The southern advantage in total chairmanships is best accounted for by the textbook theory—lack of two-party competition in the South—*and by a Republican sweep of many northern Democratic districts in the 1946 mid-term election which severely cut into the potential for northern Democratic seniority in succeeding years.*

However, the textbook theory is becoming increasingly less valid. Election data clearly show a trend toward more safe seats and more seniority for Democrats in the urban North with a parallel loss of safe Democratic seats in the rural South. The North has been recovering from the Democratic disaster of 1946, while southern seniority has fallen victim to some Republican victories, to incumbents losing in primaries, and to redistricting. The prognosis is that within a few years northern Democrats will assume greater influence in the House, and "the decline of the southerners will be accompanied by a Democratic President's greater ability to get his way with Congress."[24]

The most empirically defensible of Bickel's charges relate to the rules of debate. Certainly the filibuster offers great leverage, if not absolute control, to numerical minorities. On balance, the filibuster has historically been the tool of conservative interests. But filibusters can be stopped, as demonstrated by the successful two-thirds cloture votes on civil rights legislation in 1964, 1965, and 1968. And the filibuster has occasionally been the tool of liberal Senators. Three administration proposals in 1971 alone were affected by liberal filibusters: appropriations for supersonic transport planes, a government loan to the Lockheed Aircraft Company, and extension of the draft laws. And late in the 1972 session, filibustering liberals killed a tough anti-busing bill which had passed the House.

5. Bickel contends that a congressional constituency may vote for its congressman from a more self-centered and probably more conservative outlook than it votes for a President when it is part of a national constituency. The consequences are that the President is likely to represent a different constituency than does the House, that Congress "cannot be radically changed," and that the electoral system should "emphasize and preserve rather than seek to suppress the different orientation of the presidency."

These three conclusions emerge from an empirically unsubstantiated assertion. To suggest that self-centered and conservative attitudes motivate voters in congressional elections is to fly in the face of what is known about congressional constituencies. In their study of the 1958 congressional election—which, being mid-term, would be more likely to turn on congressional candidates and issues than would an election in a presidential year—Miller and Stokes found an abysmal ignorance of both congressional candidates and issues. Fewer than one in five respondents had read or heard anything about both candidates, well over half had read or heard nothing about either, and less than 3 percent of the voters interviewed made comments about any kind of legislative issue. Some 84 percent of the vote in 1958 was cast by party identifiers for, and on the basis of, the party affiliation of the congressional candidate. "What is more, traditional party voting is seldom connected with current legislative issues."[25] Only about 15 percent of the party identifiers mentioned current issues of public policy as reasons for what they liked and disliked about the parties.

Measured in terms of public opinion, there is no evidence that the President represents a "different constituency" than does the House, *collectively*. But even if he does, and we followed Bickel's advice to preserve the "different orientation" and different constituency for the President, then logic would dictate that this difference would be more nearly accomplished by direct election than by election through the Electoral College. Senators and Representatives are elected on the basis of imaginary lines, visible only on maps of the United States. To the extent those lines influence legislators' orientations toward public policy (and they do),[26] a different orientation for Presidents is more likely to result from sweeping aside all lines but the national borders in electing him.

Notes

1. Unless otherwise noted, the following propositions stem from these sources: Wallace Sayre and Judith Parris, VOTING FOR PRESIDENT (Washington, D.C.: The Brookings Institution, 1970), 71-73, 80-81; Alexander Bickel, REFORM AND CONTINUITY (New York: Harper Colophon Books, 1971), 5-13, 17-19; and Bickel's testimony in Hearings before the Senate Judiciary Committee on ELECTORAL COLLEGE REFORM, 91st Cong., 2nd Sess. (April 15, 16, and 17, 1970), 50. These hearings will be cited hereafter as Senate Hearings.

2. Remarks of Senator Sam Ervin in 116 CONG. REC. S16557 (daily ed., September 25, 1970), quoting from Bickel's article, "Direct Election of the President," THE NEW REPUBLIC (September 26, 1970).

3. Kevin Phillips, THE EMERGING REPUBLICAN MAJORITY (Garden City, N.Y.: Doubleday, 1970).

4. Bickel, REFORM AND CONTINUITY, 7. Sayre and Parris enter a similar disclaimer in VOTING FOR PRESIDENT, 47.

5. A Gallup poll taken in mid-October 1972 clearly indicates that Senator Edward Kennedy would have run a stronger, although still losing, race against President Nixon than did McGovern. Kennedy would have been especially potent in retaining the vote of Catholics and manual workers, whose support eroded from McGovern. (Gallup release, as published in THE SUNDAY PANTA-GRAPH [Bloomington, Ill.], November 12, 1972.)

6. Data on nonwhites, Catholics, and labor union families are from the Gallup poll press release of December 14, 1972. The data on Jews for the elections of 1952 to 1968 are from Survey Research Center findings reprinted in Hugh A. Bone, AMERICAN POLITICS AND THE PARTY SYSTEM (4th ed.; New York: McGraw-Hill, 1971), 508. The datum on Jews for 1972 is from a TIME magazine precinct study reported in TIME, November 20, 1972, 17.

7. On the greater number of voters in the suburbs than in the shrinking central cities, see U.S. Bureau of the Census, CURRENT POPULATION REPORTS, Series P-20, No. 192 "Voting and Registration in the Election of November 1968" (Washington, D.C.: Government Printing Office, 1969), 15, and the report on rapidly growing suburban counties in CONGRESSIONAL QUARTERLY WEEKLY REPORT, September 4, 1971, 1883-1889. Evidence that the growing suburban vote is predominantly, if not inexorably, Republican appears in a 1968 CBS precinct study, reported in CONGRESSIONAL QUAR-

TERLY WEEKLY REPORT, November 8, 1968, 3116, and in the CONGRES-
SIONAL QUARTERLY report on growing suburban counties cited above. See
also Hugh Bone and Austin Ranney, POLITICS AND VOTERS (3rd ed.; New
York: McGraw-Hill, 1971), 50.

8. This subsection draws heavily upon the discussion in Lawrence D.
Longley and John H. Yunker, "Who is Really Advantaged by The Electoral
College—And Who Just Thinks He Is?" a paper presented at the 67th Annual
Meeting of the American Political Science Association, Chicago, Ill., September
7-11, 1971, 9, 11-13, 16-17, and 18-21. I am indebted to Professor Longley for
sending me a manuscript draft of this paper prior to its delivery and the paper
itself after the Chicago meeting.

9. Ibid., 19. Emphasis in original.

10. Irwin Mann and L.S. Shapley, "The A Priori Voting Strength of the
Electoral College," in Martin Shubik, ed., GAME THEORY AND RELATED
APPROACHES TO SOCIAL BEHAVIOR (New York: John Wiley and Sons,
1964), 154, quoted ibid., 19.

11. For the difference coattails made in Kennedy's and Johnson's legislative
records, see Joseph Cooper and Gary Bombardier, "Presidential Leadership and
Party Success," THE JOURNAL OF POLITICS, 30 (November 1968),
1012-1027. It should be noted that this fourth point is not made by Longley
and Yunker, although it could have been. Rather, starting from the same premise
about additional votes being "power-free," they point out that stopping the
process of coalition formation exactly at the point that one has a majority
requires perfect information—a commodity in notoriously short supply in the
real world. Therefore, in their uncertainty, members of a winning coalition may
create a coalition larger than needed to insure that they do win. See Longley and
Yunker, "Who Is Really Advantaged by the Electoral College," 20, or the
companion article by John H. Yunker and Lawrence D. Longley, "The Biases of
the Electoral College: Who is Really Advantaged?", in Donald R. Matthews
(ed.), PERSPECTIVES ON PRESIDENTAL SELECTION (Washington, D.C.:
The Brookings Institution, forthcoming in 1973).

12. In interviews with Neal R. Peirce. Peirce spoke with Lawrence O'Brien,
key strategist in the Kennedy campaigns of 1960 and 1964, with Senator
Thruston B. Morton, former Republican national chairman and a member of
Nixon's 1960 campaign strategy board, and with Theodore C. Sorenson, who
had been a key Kennedy campaign adviser and white House aide. See Peirce's
THE PEOPLE'S PRESIDENT (New York: Simon and Schuster, 1968), 276-77.

13. PL 91-285, 84 Stat. 314 (1970), as described in CONGRESSIONAL
QUARTERLY WEEKLY REPORT, December 25, 1970, 3093-94.

14. THE GALLUP OPINION INDEX, August 1972, 17. This survey finding
was based on interviews with 4,149 adults aged 18 and older, conducted in June,
July, and August. The earlier study referred to was conducted in January,
February, and March of 1972.

15. V.O. Key, Jr., PUBLIC OPINION AND AMERICAN DEMOCRACY (New York: Alfred A. Knopf, 1967), Chaps. 16, 18, 19, and 21. Also see Warren Miller and Donald Stokes, "Constituency Influence in Congress," AMERICAN POLITICAL SCIENCE REVIEW, 57 (March 1963), 45-56.

16. Samuel Lubell, THE HIDDEN CRISIS IN AMERICAN POLITICS (New York: W.W. Norton, 1970), 71.

17. Lloyd Free and Hadley Cantril, THE POLITICAL BELIEFS OF AMERICANS (New York: Simon and Schuster, 1968).

18. The N's for the spectrums are slightly smaller than the N's for the samples responding to the question items given in the text above. This is because the first step in calculating both spectrums was to eliminate from consideration all respondents who answered "Don't know" to three or more of the items. For a technical description of how the five intervals in the spectrums were devised, see ibid., 207-210. The N for the Operational Spectrum is about twice as large as the N for the Ideological Spectrum because the operational items were included in both samples.

19. Lawrence H. Chamberlain, "The President, Congress, and Legislation," in Aaron Wildavsky, ed., THE PRESIDENCY (Boston: Little, Brown, 1969), 443.

20. Thomas E. Cronin, "The Textbook Presidency and Political Science," paper delivered to the 66th Annual Meeting of the American Political Science Association in Los Angeles, California, September 7-12, 1970, 31-33.

21. Cooper and Bombardier, "Presidential Leadership."

22. Bickel, REFORM AND CONTINUITY, 18-19.

23. Raymond Wolfinger and Joan Heifetz, "Safe Seats, Seniority, and Power in Congress," AMERICAN POLITICAL SCIENCE REVIEW, 59 (June 1965), 337-349, at 337.

24. Ibid., 348.

25. Miller and Stokes, "Constituency Influence in Congress," 54. Similarly, Gallup polls taken over the years tend to find that majorities or large minorities of the public do not know the name of their congressman.

26. See, e.g., Chap. 6, "Why the Senate is More Liberal than the House," in Lewis A. Froman, Jr., CONGRESSMEN AND THEIR CONSTITUENCIES (Chicago: Rand McNally, 1963), 69-84.

4

Protecting the Two-Party System

A recurrent line of argumentation is that direct election would destroy the two-party system and, consequently, would weaken the legitimacy of the Presidency. The argument grows as a tree of causality; various dysfunctional consequences branch out from a few main premises. For analytical purposes, this chapter will focus primarily on the issue of the putative growth of minor parties and the next chapter will deal with alleged threats to the sanctity of the Presidency. However, because both aspects are interrelated, the entire argument is outlined below:

I. The Electoral College and the unit rule permit the existence of only two viable parties, both of which must be broadly based geographically and politically. These two characteristics, in turn, cause:
   A. Parties to be politically moderate, which causes:
      1. Stability of government, defined as the peaceful exchange of public office and the enactment of legitimate public policy.
II. Direct election, especially with a runoff provision, would cause:
   A. A multiplicity of parties and candidates, many of which would be ideologically rigid. Such a multi-party system would cause:
      1. A pattern of runoff elections, which would cause:
         (a) Major party candidates to bargain for minor party support in the runoff. Such bargaining would cause:
            (1) Diminished legitimacy for the Presidency and . . .
            (2) Government less capable of taking decisive action, and . . .
            (3) The possibility of electing in the runoff the candidate who came in second on the first ballot. (The runner-up could also win the runoff without bargaining.) Such a "minority President" would cause:
               (i) Diminished ability of the President to govern, and . . .
               (ii) Diminished legitimacy of the electoral verdict in the eyes of the citizenry, especially if the runner-up won a runoff election which had substantially fewer voters than there were on the first ballot.
      2. If the President were elected with a 40 percent plurality on the first ballot, this would cause:
         (a) Election of a "minority President" who had been rejected by 60 percent of the voters and who may have been elected on a single

55

issue. Both conditions constitute too narrow a mandate for governing. Or . . .

(b) Secret deals with minor party candidates *before* the first ballot. Major party candidates whose chance of winning would be hurt by minor parties would make concessions to keep them out of the election; major party candidates who would be helped by minor parties would make promises to encourage them to run.

If one accepts this line of reasoning at face value, the tree of reform bears bitter fruit. However, the argument is vulnerable at virtually every point on one or both of two counts—reasonable empirical expectations of political behavior, and normative democratic theory about the kinds of functions political parties ought to perform in our society. The main emphasis in these pages will be on empirical analysis. However, some of the normative arguments will be mentioned in passing, largely because they are made by members of the United States Senate, and so presumably carry weight with some of the political actors directly charged with affecting change.

The Electoral College and the Two-Party System

The Electoral College system is composed of four fundamental components, *all four of which* are reputed to be the underpinnings for a system of two, moderate, broad-based parties. These components are election of a single man to a *single office*, by a *majority* of electoral votes, said electoral votes distributed in a fixed number to *each state*, and the states casting their votes by *unit rule*. The electoral consequences are that the candidate of only one of the two largest parties can win, that to achieve the winning majority, major party candidates must campaign in nearly all states and appeal to a wide range of minority interests to create their majority coalition, and that the resulting coalition must be both "geographically dispersed and ideologically moderate."[1]

Because of the unit rule, the argument continues, only third parties with regional strength are capable of winning any electoral votes. Third parties with a minority of popular votes nationally but without a plurality in any state are shut out of the electoral vote sweepstakes. But even electoral votes won by strong regional parties are too few in number to win the Presidency. Therefore, minority political interests must modify their demands to make them compatible with both major parties. Again, the result is a politics of moderation, accommodation, and compromise inherent in two broad-based, heterogeneous parties.

This thesis supposes a straight-line chain of causality among three variables: (1) the Electoral College unit rule is at least a necessary condition to cause (2) the two-party system, and the two-party system is at least a necessary condition to cause (3) moderation and compromise. Neither of the relationships, between the first and second variables or the second and third, are supported by empirical evidence or by the judgment of political scientists who are recognized scholars of political parties.

With respect to the first relationship, after a comprehensive survey of the works of students of political parties, the ABA Commission on Electoral College Reform found that none attribute the development of our two-party system to the Electoral College.[2] The institutions which are credited with helping to shape the two-party system are the single office of the Presidency and the single-member legislative district whose representative is elected by a plurality of the popular vote. Conversely, the consensus of scholarly opinion is that multiple parties are encouraged by multi-member legislative constituencies which elect by proportional representation, and by cabinets whose ministries can be parceled out among several legislative parties. But direct election would not change the structure of legislative elections or the single-member executive.

To be sure, potential third party movements with national as opposed to regional appeal may have been deterred by the knowledge that they would be unlikely to win any electoral votes. This knowledge also makes it difficult to aggregate the financial resources to mount a national campaign. But as Richard Goodwin testified about peace groups and civil rights groups who considered forming a third party for the 1968 election, "They have also been held back by the argument that the probable result of their effort would be to take away votes from the major party candidate closest to them in conviction, thus throwing the entire electoral vote of a state to his opponent."[3]

The same argument carries weight in a direct election under certain circumstances. A third party effort could have the dysfunctional consequence (for that party) of throwing enough of the national popular vote to the major party candidate farthest from the third party to elect him on the first ballot. Any assumption that this would *not* happen rests on the belief that a runoff election is a calculated risk. This calculation, in turn, must be derived from empirical data that with that third party in the race, the popular vote for the two major parties will be close enough and low enough that neither major party candidate can win at least 40 percent of the vote on the first ballot. Such data could be elicited from opinion polls, but the data itself might be questionable. A putative third party would have to decide *whether* to run before it committed itself to running. This decision would have to be based on polling questions which either exclude the third party from consideration, or mention it as a *speculative* party running a *speculative* candidate. All responses to such questions would be given before the actual presidential campaign began, and would, therefore, be justifiably suspect.

The point is *not* that the possibility of helping to elect the worst of two major party candidates will unalterably deter minor parties from forming. It is that it may limit the number of minor parties which do form, and it may cut into the popular vote of such parties.

The second causal linkage in the argument is that the two-party system causes moderation and compromise. However, many political scientists believe that it is just the opposite, that a two-party system is the *consequence* of moderation and compromise in the American political culture.

This premise underlies two of the four theories which attempt to explain the existence of two American parties, as summarized by Sorauf.[4] The first has already been discussed. It is the institutional theory of the single executive and the single-member legislative district with election by plurality. The second is the dualist theory. Two parties are the natural consequence of a historical duality of opposing political interests, from the early eastern financial and commercial interests opposed by western frontiersmen, to the sectional conflict over slavery and the civil war, to current divisions between urban and rural or higher and lower socioeconomic interests. Other dualistic interpretations touch on in-party versus out-party and liberal versus conservative.

The cultural theory is the third school of thought. It holds that the Anglo-American nations have developed a political culture recognizing the need for compromise, short-term pragmatism, and the avoidance of dogmatism. The fourth theory assumes that two moderate parties are the result of a fundamental social consensus. Unlike European peoples with their histories of feudalism, monarchism, religious wars, and socialist thought, Americans reached a consensus on the basic institutions of our society. With agreement on fundamentals, the political conflict that does exist is over secondary matters—means rather than ends—which permits compromise within each major party, and between them.

In appraising these four theories, Sorauf suggests that they may be as much the result of the two-party system as the cause. Once established, the two parties have a vested interest in perpetuating electoral systems hostile to minor parties, in channeling complex political demands into two alternatives, in socializing the public in the values of moderation and compromise, and in maintaining social consensus by denying a podium to dissident movements which challenge the consensus on basic American institutions.

Sorauf's last two points merit comment. It is likely that Americans reach their majority with the values of moderation, compromise, and majority rule already instilled in them by the socialization process of family, schools, and voluntary associations. To assume that a young adult sheds his dogmatism and replaces it with moderation upon the act of registering to vote or identifying with a party is to assume that parties create instant social values. It is more likely that parties both reflect and reinforce values already extant. Which leads to Sorauf's last point. To be sure, major parties deny their good offices to radical dissenters from the fundamental consensus. Failure to do so would result in losing elections and very likely the demise of any major party that acted otherwise. Communists and Socialists have lost elections as separate parties precisely because Democrats are not about to lose elections for them, as well as because most Democrats adhere to capitalistic principles. Similarly, Birchites and the American Nazi Party are separate political entities because the Republicans, as a party, not only disagree with their positions but would become extinct as a party if they did not.

Inferentially, Sorauf is cognizant of these factors, for he finally opts for the consensus theory as the main independent variable which allows the others to interact.

If the preceding discussion appears far removed from electoral votes and the unit rule, that only serves to demonstrate that "the suggestion that the two-party system is primarily or even significantly sustained by the Electoral College seems to be a classic case of putting the cart before the horse."[5]

Direct Election and Minor Parties

In addition to the discredited argument that the Electoral College is the underpinning of our two-party system, those who fear the rise of minor parties base their predictions on four models: New York state, southern Democratic primaries, continental Europe, especially France, and splinter parties.

In varying degrees, all four models compare unfavorably to more reasonable estimates of future partisan developments under direct election. The interrelated questions that must be asked are: What is the likelihood that one or more minor parties will become quadrennial institutions? And if institutionalized, what are such parties likely to accomplish?

Minor Parties in New York

Since World War II, New York has had a viable Liberal party. By holding a balance of power in close elections, the Liberals have influenced the choice of candidates and policies of the Democrats. In the last few years, a Conservative party has emerged to follow a similar strategy with respect to the Republican party. Direct election, we are told, would infect the national body politic with the multi-party virus of New York. Unable to win with their own candidates for President, minor parties could exercise disproportionate influence by determining which major party candidates win or lose.

Extrapolating New York's history to the nation's future overlooks some obvious incongruities. The fact that New York is the only state with viable minor parties suggests that their existence can be attributed to conditions peculiar to New York. That is precisely the point made by a man in a position to know, U.S. Senator James Buckley of New York, elected in 1970 on the Conservative party ticket. In a televised interview with his brother, Senator Buckley expressed a strong preference for a two-party system and recommended against the spread of minor parties to other states. Senator Buckley attributed the need for a Conservative party in *his state* to the Liberal party's influence in making both major parties gravitate in a leftward direction. But this need, in turn, results from conditions endemic to New York. According to Buckley, that state does not have a viable primary election system for statewide office; therefore, it is not feasible for conservative Republicans like him to fight for control within the Republican party structure. Also, Buckley attributes the success of the Liberal party to unusual conditions. Its ability to maintain continuity and organization over a long period is possible because the party is composed primarily of members and officers of other existing institutions, two labor unions based in New York City. Union officials and the ongoing union organization therefore handle the continual paper work and other demanding details of political party organization. Finally, highly competent union leaders, e.g., Alex Rose of the International Ladies Garment Workers Union, play a dual role as able Liberal party leaders.[6]

Southern Primaries

That political conditions unique to New York account for its minor parties is corroborated by the fact that those parties exist despite the absence of runoff elections, not because of them. Therefore, those who contend that runoffs encourage minor parties must shift their geographical and political grounds from general elections in New York to Democratic primaries in the South. This is done with great aplomb, invariably by referring to Key's classic *Southern Politics*, but ignoring its content. Thus, Bickel feels free to write that with direct election,

There would be *little inducement to unity in each party* at or following the conventions. Everything would be preparation for later coalitions. We would see on a national scale the kind of *unstructured politics* that characterized much of the *single party South* in its heyday, and that still characterizes some of it. The *real election was the Democratic primary*, which would regularly draw several candidates, some intent on no more than obtaining, say, the Commissionership of Agriculture through a judicious *later bargain.* The candidates sorted themselves out between the first vote and the runoff. Two or four years thence, *everything started afresh.*[7] (Emphasis added.)

Deferring the matter of bargaining for later consideration, we can now emphasize that Democratic party disunity in its own party primary is a luxury that cannot be afforded in the context of a general election for President with strong Republican competition. The same, of course, applies to Republicans facing Democratic competition in a general election. Indeed, one of Key's *major findings* about southern politics was that even within the context of Democratic primaries, the degree of unity in a state Democratic party and the extent to which it maintained continuity of leadership over time was in almost direct proportion to the competition offered by the Republican party. Key found the most cohesive Democratic parties—those with only a major and a minor faction—in Virginia, North Carolina, and Tennessee; states with at least a modicum of Republican opposition. "The cohesiveness of the majority faction in these states points to the extraordinary influence of even a small opposition party. . . . In all three states Republican opposition contributes to the creation of one tightly organized Democratic faction."[8]

The southern model of disunity falls short on a second critical dimension. Presidential minor parties are to be feared, we are told, because they would be ideologically hidebound and issue-oriented. The prognosis is for at least four parties covering the ideological spectrum: New Left, Democratic, Republican, and a Wallace-type party of the Right. However, Key found that the most faction-ridden southern Democratic primaries, those with the greatest number of candidates fracturing the first ballot vote, were contested on issueless and ideologically-free bases. The main causal factor for multiple candidacies, Key found, was simply localism. Almost any citizen who cared to run for Governor could poll a big vote from his "friends and neighbors." This pattern, with some variation among states depending on whether a figure with statewide recognition was running, e.g., a Ferguson in Texas or a Bilbo in Mississippi, was present in the three most faction-ridden states Key studied—Texas, Mississippi, and Florida. The low salience of issues and ideology in the primaries of these states is exemplified by the comment of a north Florida county judge, who observed: "Issues? Why, son, they don't have a damn thing to do with it."

Key attempted to grapple with the hypothesis that the legal possibility of a primary runoff causes multi-factionalism (many candidates in the first ballot primary). While election by plurality requires factions to unite before the election, in a runoff situation each factional candidate can take his chance that his vote, however small, may be sufficient to place him in the runoff. "Like many beautiful theories," Key wrote, "the truth of the general idea is hard to determine."[9] One could, he observed, compare Virginia and Tennessee—states without runoffs—to other states with runoffs, and conclude that plurality election foists greater party unity upon Virginia and Tennessee. But this conclusion would ignore such other variables as the sizable minority of Republican voters in those states, as well as in North Carolina, to which Key attributes Democratic cohesion. He also finds Arkansas an exception to the hypothesis, for that state's factionalism more closely approximated a dual form *since* the adoption of the runoff in 1939 than before. Also, the New Deal had some effect on Arkansas' factional structure.

European Elections:
Austria and France

When left to his own devices, an opponent of direct election may conjure up as many political parties as there are professional football teams. Professor Black of the Yale Law School asks why we may not expect 10 or 20 parties. Each, as in France, with a special mission, a special issue, instead of the present situation which promotes accommodation within the framework of two parties.[10]

As we shall see, this model of French politics is as inaccurate for contemporary France as it would be for the United States. In both cases the reason is the same: *direct election to a single office cannot sustain a plethora of parties because the total popular vote does not fragment in even rough proportion to the number of parties in an election.* The creation of 10 parties would no more mean that each would receive approximately 10 percent of the vote than the existence of five parties means that each would poll approximately 20 percent of the vote.

Why? Because most issues and most candidates are perceived by the electorate as falling into a relatively few clusters, and the popular vote that mobilizes behind each cluster is finite and of approximately constant size. A left and a right and a middle constituency of voters are not like accordians. They do not expand to accommodate additional candidates. They are like pies. Each additional candidate seeking a share of the left bloc pie means *either* that each left candidate receives a smaller slice of pie, *or* that the most popular one or two candidates of the left will divide the pie between them. The same is true of candidates in the middle and the right. Therefore, in the context of American politics, we might expect the Democrats and Republicans to continue sharing the large electoral constituency of the middle with, *at most*, one candidate for each of the much smaller right and left constituencies.[11]

To the extent this analysis is valid, and to the extent it is heeded by political elites, we would expect a relatively high degree of accommodation. Those on the moderate left and on the moderate right could be expected to retain their traditional membership in the Democratic and Republican parties, respectively. Those on the extreme left and extreme right would have to unite behind one candidate each, if they choose to run their own candidates at all.

The foregoing propositions are supported by empirical data from presidential elections in Austria and France. Since World War II, Austria has held five direct elections of its President, the first in 1951, the most recent in 1971. An absolute majority of popular votes is required for election, with a runoff if necessary. Only in the first election of 1951, which had six candidates on the first ballot, was there a runoff election. In the four succeeding elections there was a winner on the first ballot because only the two major parties ran candidates, despite the fact that at least three, and sometimes four, parties held seats in the Austrian parliament.

The Austrian case not only demonstrates the paucity of minor party candidates in direct presidential elections, but also the need for minor parties to accommodate themselves to the major party closest to them in the political spectrum. The two major parties in the 1951 election were the People's Party and the Socialists. While neither party's candidate received a majority on the first ballot, the People's Party candidate had a 1 percent plurality over the Socialist. Between the first ballot and the runoff, the Communist party instructed its people to vote for the Socialist candidate, who won the runoff with 52.1 percent of the total vote. Socialists have defeated People's Party candidates in two-way presidential elections ever since.

In 1962, the French Constitution was amended to provide for direct election of the President by an absolute majority of the popular vote. Two elections have been held under that provision, in 1965 and 1969. Table 4-1 displays the vote polled by each candidate in those elections. Although both elections had no less than six candidates in the field, and both were decided in a runoff two weeks after the first ballot, these elections demonstrate the principle of marginal candidates sharing the same small constituencies. In both elections, about 90 percent of the total vote on the first ballot was captured by the top three

Table 4-1

Percent of Popular Vote Polled in French Presidential Elections of 1965 and 1969

Candidate	First Ballot		Second Ballot
Election of December 5 and 19, 1965			
De Gaulle (Gaullist)	44.6%		55.2%
Mitterand (Left Federation)	31.7	91.9%	44.8
Lecanuet (Democratic Center)	15.6		
Tixier-Vignancour (Extreme Right)	5.2		
Marcilhacy	1.7		
Barbu	1.2		
Election of June 1 and 15, 1969			
Pompidou (Gaullist)	44.0%		57.6%
Poher (Centrist)	23.4	88.9%	42.2
Duclos (Communist)	21.5		
Defferre (Socialist-SFIO)	5.1		
Rocard (Unified Socialist-PSU)	3.7		
Ducatel	1.3		
Krivine (Trotskyite)	1.1		

Source: Lowell G. Noonan, FRANCE: THE POLITICS OF CONTINUITY AND CHANGE (New York: Holt, Rinehart, and Winston, 1970), 262, 452.

candidates, representing what passes in France for the established party alignments of the left, middle, and moderate conservative.

A second lesson of the French elections is that neither would have required a runoff if 40 percent of the vote, rather than an absolute majority, were sufficient for election. In both elections the top candidate on the first ballot polled a comfortable 44 percent of the vote (higher than Nixon's 43 percent in 1968). Given that multiple parties are a far stronger political tradition in France than in the United States, the French experience does not support the contention that direct election in this country will either foment numerous parties, or that if formed, such parties would succeed in creating a pattern of runoff elections. As a spokesman for the U.S. Chamber of Commerce envisioned the future under direct election, a few splinter parties would form in the first few elections. But these parties would fail to cause a runoff, "and their adherents will determine thereafter never again to waste their votes."

That viable minor parties are not necessarily the consequence of runoff elections is demonstrated by the states of Arkansas, Georgia, Rhode Island, and Texas. These states require election by absolute majority both in their primary *and general elections*, with runoffs if no candidate achieves a majority.[12] All four states are in the mainstream of two-party competition.

Splinter Candidates and Spoilers

Some opponents of direct election insist that any or all seekers of the Presidency who failed of nomination in their party's convention would run as splinter party candidates, either to play the spoiler role by denying the prize to the party that refused to nominate them, or to hope for a deadlock on the first ballot and play kingmaker by bargaining with the two front-runners for splinter party support in the runoff. The premise is that splinter candidates rarely run now because of their inability to carry enough states under the unit rule provision of the Electoral College.

This bare bones theory then speculates about what might have happened in 1968, or what could happen in the future, under a direct election system. Some opponents of direct election hypothesize that the three candidates in 1968 might have been joined by others who failed of nomination in the major party conventions. The field might have included Eugene McCarthy and John V. Lindsay to the left of Humphrey, Nelson Rockefeller to the left of Nixon and Ronald Reagan to his right, along with George Wallace. Almost the same cast of characters would fit a 1972 scenario, with the addition of Republicans Pete McCloskey and John Ashbrook, and Democrats Edward Kennedy, Edmund Muskie, and George McGovern.

The pertinent but purely speculative questions are: Would any of these hypothetical splinter candidates actually have run in a direct election in 1968?

And *if* any had run, would that have effected a deadlock on the first ballot by denying either Nixon or Humphrey 40 percent of the vote? Finally, even if there had been a deadlock and a runoff election, what difference would that have made? The rest of this chapter will address itself to the first two questions. The third question will be considered in the next chapter.

To name a host of putative seekers of a party's nomination is not equivalent to listing a roster of candidates in the general election. For one thing, not all nominal "candidates" for the nomination really expect to receive it, or announce their "availability" with that goal in mind. They may simply be engaging in a dry run for the nomination four years in the future. Or they may hope—as did McCloskey and Ashbrook in 1972—to exert influence over the platform or the policy position of their party's nominee. They may even "run" to retain the political leadership of their states' delegations, or to prevent front-runners from entering their home state presidential primary and causing divisiveness in the state party. Reagan's 1968 "candidacy" kept everyone but himself out of the California Republican primary, and may have achieved in some degree some of the other goals of quasi-candidates.

A second damper on splinter candidacies is that the Rockefellers and the Reagans, the Kennedys, the Humphreys, and even the McCarthys, are professional politicians, with more than a modicum of party loyalty. The pattern in both parties is for internecine strife before the nomination, then a rallying 'round the party's banner after it. Thre are exceptions, e.g., Theodore Roosevelt's conviction that the nomination was "stolen" from him at the Republican convention of 1912, the Progressive Party and Dixiecrat candidacies in 1948, and Wallace's insurgency in 1968. But by and large, politicians of *national stature* in both parties support—or do not overtly oppose—their party's standard bearer.

In addition to an abstract sense of party loyalty, those who lose a nomination also support their party's candidate because (and if) he is the clear choice of a majority of the party's rank-and-file voters in the nation. This is not only obeisance to the normative doctrine of majority rule, but a realistic recognition that candidates who cannot command a large majority of their own partisans cannot win an election even with their party's nomination, no less without it.

With respect to the 1968 nominations, after a careful analysis of opinion polls taken just before the conventions, Scammon and Wattenberg conclude that Humphrey and Nixon were far and away the favorites of Democratic and Republican voters, respectively.[13] In 1972, Nixon remained the overwhelming choice for renomination among Republicans, while McGovern edged Humphrey and Wallace as the candidate preferred by a plurality of Democrats responding to a Gallup poll conducted prior to the Democratic convention.[14]

All these factors cast considerable doubt on the allegation that many splinter candidates would have entered a direct election in 1968 or, having entered, could have effected a deadlock. Certainly Nixon's candidacy was the least likely to be threatened by defections from his own party. Neither Rockefeller nor Reagan had sufficient reason, or sufficient popular following, to oppose him. Moreover, once the Republican party nominated Nixon, large numbers of those Republicans who previously favored Reagan or Rockefeller would have shifted their support to Nixon—even if he had been opposed by one or both of the former as splinter candidates. *Party loyalty plays its role among the rank-and-file as well as among political activists.*[15] Most of the voters that Nixon actually *did* lose were disgruntled Democrats who preferred Nixon to Humphrey, but who voted for Wallace. Similarly, much of McCarthy's early support (which was more anti-Johnson than pro-McCarthy) dissipated late in the campaign, but crystallized as electoral support for Wallace.[16] In short, Nixon's 43 percent of the popular vote, enough to win a direct election on the first ballot, looks pretty stable in retrospect.

But even failing a deadlock, might splinter candidates not run with the minimal expectations of playing the spoiler? The answer is not an unqualified yes, for there are both institutional and motivational factors that enter the picture.

On the institutional side, a spoiler candidate is most likely to achieve his goal in a direct election only if the two major party candidates are in a close race. But this is precisely when a spoiler is likely to be effective under the Electoral College. If, for example, Eugene McCarthy had wanted to punish the Humphrey forces by throwing the election to Nixon in 1968, he could have accomplished it with virtual certainty simply by filing for election in New York state and giving all that state's electoral votes to the Republican candidate, much as Henry Wallace did in 1948. But in 1968 the McCarthy forces were not motivated to attempt a spoiler role.

They were not motivated because there are only four reasons that, singly or in combination, prompt a splinter candidate to run. These reasons are quite independent of the form of the election, whether direct or Electoral College, and none were sufficiently salient to the liberal wing of either party in 1968. The four motivations for a splinter candidacy are:

1. The splinter candidate feels that he is really the popular choice of his party's rank-and-file for the nomination, but that the nomination was "stolen" from him by machinations in his party's convention.

2. As a result of the first reason, the splinter candidate believes he might win the election if he runs.

3. The splinter candidate represents a wing of his party which is ideologically closer to the other major party than to the wing of his party which succeeded in nominating its leader. Therefore, in terms of public policy, the splinter candidate may countenance, or even prefer, a victory of the other major party's candidate over the candidate of his former party.

4. The splinter candidate represents a shade of political opinion so extreme

that it is beyond the mainstream of either major party. Therefore, the candidacy is mounted as an ideologically doctrinaire protest against both parties. Perhaps there is also the belief that a good showing in the election will move at least one of the major parties closer to the position of the minor party during the election campaign, after the election, or in the next election. In some toxologies, minor parties that form largely from this motivation may as properly be considered "doctrinal-ideological" as "splinter-secessionist."[17]

The first and third reasons almost certainly motivated the Bull Moose candidacy of Theodore Roosevelt in 1912, and the second also may have been present. The Dixiecrats of 1948 were clearly motivated by the fourth reason, and possibly by the third. The fourth reason is the only tenable explanation of Henry Wallace's pro-Soviet candidacy for the Progressive party in 1948. Finally, George Wallace's 1968 campaign was in the same tradition as the Dixiecrat rebellion of 1948 and was probably motivated primarily by the same reason, the fourth, with overtones of the third.

But none of the reasons were salient for Democratic doves in 1968. Despite the self-perpetuating rhetoric about "boss rule" at the Democratic convention (like football teams, political factions like to "psych themselves up" for the big game), the opinion poll findings clearly demonstrate that Humphrey did not "steal the nomination" from McCarthy, and McCarthy had to know this. Nor could McCarthy or his supporters conceivably have found Nixon's policies more palatable than Humphrey's. To reiterate Goodwin's statement, one of the reasons the McCarthy forces did not enter the general election was a fear of throwing electoral votes to Nixon.

Nor was the McCarthy faction outside the mainstream of the Democratic party. Their only *policy* difference with the administration forces at the convention was over the wording of the Vietnam plank. The administration plank agreed to halt the bombing of North Vietnam contingent on some degree of lessened hostilities by North Vietnam, and favored free elections in South Vietnam after the war. The minority "peace plank" pledged unconditional cessation of bombing and favored a negotiated (not elected) coalition government in Saigon that would include the National Liberation Front. That the minority plank was hardly radical is indicated by the fact that it received 40 percent of the votes at the convention, while McCarthy and McGovern together polled only 29 percent of the vote on the first, and only, presidential nominating ballot. Moreover, later in the campaign, Humphrey moved toward the minority position, first by announcing that he would have found "no difficulty" in accepting the minority plank, and later by announcing his willingness, if elected, to risk a cessation of bombing. Five days before the election, that is exactly what President Johnson did do. The McCarthyites affected the issue positions taken in the campaign and the acts of an incumbent President without running their own candidate (although they could not predict they would be successful).

The lesson of 1968, as of other presidential years, is that splinter parties neither spring forth nor die *primarily* because of the electoral system. Although the method of aggregating and assigning votes has some influence as an independent variable, of more importance are the perceptions of the degree of political deprivation inherent in a two-party structure. These perceptions may or may not be sufficient to motivate insurgent candidates, depending on the particular political circumstances at the time. The circumstances of the Republican convention of 1912 varied greatly, in degree and in kind, from the situation at the Democratic convention of 1968. Their own rhetoric notwithstanding, professional politicans invariably make more intelligent appraisals of political conditions than do some students of politics, or intellectual dilettantes who spend more time writing about politics than observing it, more time prescribing political norms than researching political behavior.

Whatever Happened to Parties
as the Voice of the People?

Shifting the perspective from empirical analysis to normative prescription, the case against multiple parties can be faulted for the implications it has for the role of political parties in democratic theory. Minor parties with a strong regional base, such as the Dixiecrats in 1948 or southern slates of uncommitted electors, are unquestionably advantaged under the unit rule provisions of the Electoral College, but would have less electoral impact under direct election. Conversely, minor parties with an electoral base insufficiently concentrated to carry even a single state, but which might poll a respectable percentage of the nationwide popular vote, would benefit by direct election. In short, the two types of minor party, regionally-based or nationally-based, are not on a common footing under the Electoral College. Nor would they be under direct election. The normative question, then, turns on whether presidential elections should be open to the possibility of influence by nationwide forces of discontent (liberal, conservative, or both), or by regional ones (deep southern opposition to integration).

A preference and justification for nationwide minor parties was expressed by Republican Senator Howard Baker of Tennessee in Senate debate. Under the 40 percent direct election plan, he observed, a minor party might poll up to 10 or 20 percent of the vote. But if it did, it would not be a small party; the Republican party was even smaller in 1856. Therefore, he concluded, there ought to be room for splinter parties that can poll that large a vote nationally, *but not regionally*. A purely regional party can possibly throw an election into the House of Representatives, but regionalism, he insisted, is wrong. The 40 percent rule recognizes the legitimacy of national splinter parties.

So too, indirectly, does the runoff provision. In criticizing the contingency provisions of the Griffin-Tydings plan, which would preclude a runoff election,

Baker argued that Congress has no right to attempt to legislate out of existence efforts by third parties. Third parties prosper or fail in "direct relationship to the effectiveness of the job that the two national parties do in seeking out and determining the views of the people and translating them into effective policies for government." Under direct election, Baker observed, the major parties will simply have to become more responsible in competing for every vote.

Similar sentiments were expressed by former Senator Fred Harris of Oklahoma, who informed his Senate colleagues: " . . . I do not fear that the political system in America is so weak that to allow the people to express their will will destroy it. I would say, if that will destroy it, then perhaps it is destroyed already."

The sentiments of Senators Baker and Harris can be expressed in more precise, empirical terms. The probability of a runoff being required is a function of the dispersion of the vote among three or more parties on the first ballot. The degree of dispersion, in turn, reflects the degree of political dissensus in the polity. Consequently, if there were a runoff election, *the runoff would not be a cause of political dissatisfaction and instability, but a reflection and manifestation of them.* Different types of electoral and party systems vary in the form and to the extent to which they permit socialization of conflict. But despite these variations, any electoral/party system which consistently chokes off legitimate grievances and, by so doing, prevents their resolution by the political system, is engendering a future spasm of outraged reaction in exchange for a false sense of temporary tranquility. A political system is like a kettle of boiling water and the electoral/party system is analogous to its cover. The cover does not cause the heat. But it can contain a safety valve which slowly but consistently lets off the accumulated steam, or it can remorselessly clamp down on the constantly expanding force until the explosion.

We now turn to the question of what difference it would make if the President did have to be elected in a runoff.

Notes

1. Senate Report No. 91-1123, 91st Cong., 2nd Sess., Judiciary Committee, "Direct Popular Election of the President" (August 14, 1970), 31. Hereafter cited as Senate Report.

2. The scholarly works consulted were those by Goodman, Grum, Holcombe, Key, Penniman, Rossiter, Schattschneider, Sindler, Sharp, and Duverger. (See comment by Senator Birch Bayh of Indiana in Hearings before the Senate Judiciary Committee on ELECTORAL COLLEGE REFORM, 91st Cong., 2nd Sess. [April 15, 16, and 17, 1970], 93, hereafter cited as Senate Hearings, and ELECTING THE PRESIDENT: A REPORT OF THE COMMISSION ON ELECTORAL COLLEGE REFORM of the American Bar Association [January

1967], 5, note 2, hereafter cited as ABA Report. The ABA Report is reprinted in the appendix to Senate Hearings, 291-348.)

3. Senate Hearings, 80, 93.

4. Frank Sorauf, PARTY POLITICS IN AMERICA (2nd ed.; Boston: Little, Brown, 1972), 37-40.

5. Neal R. Peirce, THE PEOPLE'S PRESIDENT (New York: Simon and Schuster, 1968), 261.

6. "Firing Line," PBS telecast, August 18, 1971, William F. Buckley, Jr. interview with Senator James Buckley.

7. Alexander Bickel, REFORM AND CONTINUITY (New York: Harper Colophon Books, 1971), 24-25.

8. V.O. Key, Jr., SOUTHERN POLITICS (New York: Random House Vintage Books, 1949), 300.

9. Ibid., 420.

10. Senate Hearings, 143.

11. On the essentially moderate-middle political orientation of most Americans, see, e.g., Richard Scammon and Ben Wattenberg, THE REAL MAJORITY (New York: Coward-McCann, 1970); V.O. Key, Jr., PUBLIC OPINION AND AMERICAN DEMOCRACY (New York: Alfred A. Knopf, 1961); and Samuel Lubell, THE HIDDEN CRISIS IN AMERICAN POLITICS (New York: W.W. Norton, 1970). As Scammon and Wattenberg observe, the middle in American politics may move from year to year, but most voters move with it (p. 78).

12. Remarks of Senator Bayh in 116 CONG. REC. S15142 (daily ed., September 10, 1970).

13. Scammon and Wattenberg, REAL MAJORITY, 148-49.

14. CONGRESSIONAL QUARTERLY WEEKLY REPORT, July 15, 1972, 1778.

15. This is a well-established generalization from political research. The older the partisan, e.g., the longer he has voted for and identified with the same party, the more likely he is to continue to vote for his party's candidates. This is why a disproportionate number of Wallace voters outside the South were under 30. (See Philip E. Converse and others, "Continuity and Change in American Politics: Parties and Issues in the 1968 Election," THE AMERICAN POLITICAL SCIENCE REVIEW, 63 [December 1969], 1103-04.)

16. Ibid., 1091-93.

17. See Hugh A. Bone, AMERICAN POLITICS AND THE PARTY SYSTEM (4th ed.; New York: McGraw-Hill, 1971), 86.

5

Protecting the Presidency: Runoffs, Bargaining, and Illegitimacy

Direct election is impugned as an invitation to back-room bargaining for the White House and to electing the second choice of the nation's voters. With contributions from both liberals and conservatives, this indictment becomes a stirring chord of argumentation. But as we hope to demonstrate, close inspection reveals the argumentation to be false.

Runoffs and Bargaining

Drawing on the model of democratic primaries in the South, some opponents of direct election insist that the period between the first ballot and the runoff would be a time of unsavory bargaining. Minor party candidates eliminated on the first ballot would extract promises and concessions from one or both of the two front-runners in exchange for delivering their blocs of voters to them in the runoff.[1] But since the southern model is not sufficiently disturbing in its implications, the predictions go well beyond it. Bargaining advantages would accrue to a variety of minor party extremists, to a black separatist party,[2] "to demagogues, to quick-cure medicine men, and to fascists of left and right."

The runoff election would become divisive and bitter, it is argued, for the candidate who came in second on the first ballot would court the extremists, the racial, or dogmatic voting groups. His only chance to win the runoff would be to win their votes, and in seeking them he would change the tone of the campaign. The very bargaining process itself would assume an aura of sinister secrecy. Under the present system, interest groups bargain with aspirants for the Presidency, but "The coalition supporting the nominees is now developed in the reasonably open processes of preconvention and convention politics and is well publicized during the days when the delegates are gathered together. . . . " With a runoff, presidential selection would return to the "smoke-filled rooms" of the past.

These predictions ignore an inherent problem in "secret" bargains over issues and ideological precepts. If the concessions wrung from a major party candidate are kept secret, the minor party candidate has no grounds on which to publicly urge his followers to vote for that candidate. The more extreme the demands of the minor party, the more it would have to explicate the nature of the prize it was won to its members. For example, since many of the followers of George Wallace are presumably opposed to integration through school busing, Wallace's

71

public endorsement of any other candidate would have to enlighten Wallace voters about that candidate's position on that issue. Similarly, any black separatist party would have to tell *its* members why they should choose one white man over another in the runoff.

It is precisely because the coalition for a runoff requires the active participation of huge segments of the entire electorate that electoral politics are perhaps the most aboveboard of any. By contrast, coalition formation in legislative bodies and in nominating conventions involve, at most, a few hundreds of members, most of whom are socialized in the sometime secret ways of professional politicians. It was on these grounds that in 1970 a majority of the Senate Judiciary Committee deemed a runoff the "most appropriate contingency in a situation where the country is so divided that no candidate receives 40 percent of the popular vote. The Committee reasoned that no other contingency procedure would insure as much legitimacy and would be less susceptible to intrigue and closed-door deals."

But secrecy aside, the argument is made that two minor party candidates, "one regional and one ideological," could poll close to 20 percent of the vote. This would put them in an enviable bargaining position to offer their votes to a major party candidate, either before the first ballot (thus ensuring his election on it) or before the runoff. Either way, the runoff provision

. . . opens the door to public political bargaining with the most far-reaching consequences. Concessions wrung from major party candidates either before or after the first election would be made in a heated atmosphere conducive to the creation of public distrust. Given the fact bargaining before the runoff election would take place under conditions of division and disappointment, cynical political moves might in themselves lead to a crisis of respect and legitimacy in the selection of the President.[3]

This hypothetical illegitimacy is one reason for claiming that the President would be incapable of governing. Another is that in a multi-candidate situation consensus candidates would be at a disadvantage. Each electoral faction would unite behind the candidate who expressed most clearly its parochial view. Support for middle-of-the-road candidates would consequently dry up on the first ballot, *perhaps to the point where they would be excluded from the runoff.* With two extremist candidates in the runoff, the winner would be unable to produce a consensus and, therefore, would be incapable of governing the nation.

But middle-of-the-road electoral support would dry up *only* if a majority of the electorate were no longer middle-of-the-road. Two extremist candidates could come in first and second on the first ballot only if the overwhelming majority of the voters were, themselves, polarized into two extreme groups, each holding intensely to irreconcilable positions. But this is the stuff of which civil wars are made; its peaceful resolution lies outside the capacity of any democracy.[4] Moreover, so high a degree of political volatility is neither caused nor permanently retarded by anything as superficial as the *way* we elect our Presidents. The chronic error in this line of argument is the assumption that a particular form of electoral structure dampens explosive political attitudes, much as carbon rods inserted into an atomic pile prevent critical mass.

Constraints on Bargaining

Any intelligent appraisal of the nature and consequences of runoff elections, then, must be based on the character of the electorate, and of political parties, as we now know them. The central characteristics of both are moderation and pragmatism. Given these operational values, the amount of mischief that a runoff election could foment is severely limited by the constraints placed on the ability of both major and minor parties to bargain with each other.

Consider the charge that the major party candidate who comes in second on the first ballot would strike bargains with extremist parties before the runoff, or even that both major party candidates would compete for the fringe or extremist vote. We define fringe or extremist parties in the conventional sense as those whose demands are contradictory to the wishes of a majority of voters. Both candidates in the runoff would be constrained against bowing to these demands by the fear of losing large segments of the moderate voters, Republican or Democratic, who voted for them on the first ballot. *And the more extreme the minor party demands, the less a major party candidate could accede to them without alienating his first ballot supporters in the runoff.*

There is historical precedent to support this conclusion. In 1896 the Democrats nominated William Jennings Bryan, who got the support of the Populists but lost the election disastrously. Indeed, the election of 1896 relegated the Democrats to clearly minority status in the nation for a generation. And in the 1968 campaign, both major party candidates pledged they would not deal with George Wallace for his electors if neither of them received a majority in the Electoral College.

A different set of circumstances would prevail if a minor party were moderate, rather than extreme, in its demands. We can define a "moderate" minor party as one whose demands are favored by a minority of voters (the minor party voters) and are *not opposed* by a substantial minority or by a majority of voters. *But these kinds of demands are precisely the ones that a majority party would rationally adopt as part of its own program.* By so doing, the majority party adds the putative minor party voters to its electoral coalition without erosion of other coalition members. In certain circumstances, a majority party might even accept a position on an issue which is favored by a minority but opposed by a larger minority or by a majority. This would be the kind of position favored by a "passionate minority," one for which major party support on that issue is more important than the major party's stand on all other issues.[5]

The issue position would also have to be opposed by an "unpassionate" majority, i.e., the intensity of opposition by a majority of voters must be low enough that the major party's stand on that issue is of less importance to the majority than the party's position on other issues.

It is in this manner that, historically, major parties have accrued new members to their coalition and, in so doing, have swallowed up the *raison d'etre* of moderate minor parties. As Senator James Eastland points out:

Traditionally, these parties have disappeared because one or both of the major parties would embrace in whole or in part the issue advocated by the supporters of the splinter party, or because social or economic conditions which caused the emergence of this issue changed. We can expect this to hold true in the future.[6]

There are also constraints on the capacity of issue-oriented, ideological minor parties to bargain with major party candidates. No minor party can really hold a balance of power position in a runoff election unless it can "deliver" its voters with *equal ease to either major party*. This would be possible *only if both major party candidates and major party platforms were equally agreeable or disagreeable to it*. But in the context of American politics, this is patently absurd. How effectively could a black party bargain with a Humphrey, a McGovern, or a Kennedy by threatening that it would tell its members to vote for a Nixon or an Agnew in a runoff? Or by threatening to instruct its voters not to vote in the runoff? In either case, Nixon or Agnew would win. It would be equally difficult for someone like George Wallace to threaten Nixon that Wallace supporters could be "delivered" in the runoff to some northern, liberal Democrat. Clearly, except for rabid revolutionary theorists—whose doctrine is that things must get worse (to precipitate the revolution) before they get better—any splinter group rationally must vote for the major party candidate whose ideological position is closest to it. To vote for the other major party, or to refrain from voting, is irrational. It accepts the *greater* of two evils.

. The corollary constraint is that *minor party candidates are unable to "deliver" their voters to any candidate or party that those voters do not wish to vote for*. In the words of Senator Eastland, an opponent of S.J. Res. 1:

It is unrealistic and unreasonable to think that the candidate of such a splinter party [one created to advocate an issue], or its leaders, could instruct their followers how to vote in a runoff election. These people voted on the issues in the first election, and they would vote on the issues in the runoff election. They would vote for the major party candidate in the runoff election who more nearly embraced their ideas and expressed their feelings. . . .

Our whole political history suggests that even in personality-oriented elections it is very hazardous for an eliminated candidate to advise his supporters which of two remaining candidates to support. The normal human reaction is to resent such instruction.[7]

Senator Eastland is joined by two other opponents of direct election, Senator Ervin and Richard Goodwin, who (perhaps in an unguarded moment) also expressed doubt that political leaders can "deliver" their supporters.

A few electoral vignettes (they will be described too briefly to be called case studies) offer empirical corroboration of these two generalizations: (1) dissident elements throw their electoral support to the major party candidate closest to them in his political orientation, and (2) candidates have great difficulty in delivering their voters to other candidates.

The 1971 Mississippi democratic gubernatorial primary nicely illustrates both generalizations. Charles Evers, Mayor of Fayette, Mississippi and a nationally-publicized civil rights leader, was the first black man in the history of Mississippi to run for Governor. He appeared on the general election ballot as the candidate of the "loyalist" Democrats of Mississippi, an integrated group recognized as the "official" Democratic party of the state by the Democratic National Committee. As the candidate of a separate party, Evers did not enter the primary of the regular Democratic party. Of the six candidates who did, two—Jimmy Swan and Marshall Perry—ran on strictly racial appeals. The other candidates were, by Mississippi standards, moderates, perhaps in part because some 280,000 blacks were registered for the 1971 primary, a significant increase from the 180,000 registered in 1967 and the 25,000 registered in 1963. One candidate, Lt. Governor Charles Sullivan, even promised to place blacks in state jobs if elected. However, Evers urged Mississippi blacks to vote for the segregationist, Swan, on the grounds that he would be easier for Evers to defeat in the general election.

Most observers believed this was far too great a risk for blacks to take, that black voters would support Sullivan. These observers were correct. On the first ballot, Sullivan won almost 39 percent of the vote, second place went to William Waller (also a racial moderate) with 29 percent, and Swan finished a poor third with 16 percent (104,000 votes). The remaining 16 percent of the vote split fairly evenly among the other four candidates, with Perry, the other segregationist, polling less than 3 percent. Considering that something over 644,000 votes were cast on the first ballot, it would appear that few of the 280,000 registered blacks heeded Evers' plea to vote for an avowed segregationist. Not many whites did, either. Waller went on to defeat Sullivan in the runoff, a campaign centered on nonracial issues.

In the general election for Governor, Waller defeated Evers by some 528,000 votes (77 percent) to 151,000 (22 percent), with the remaining 1 percent of the vote going to another independent candidate. Although an unusually high turnout of white voters reportedly swelled Waller's margin, Evers' 151,000 votes was not much more than half of the 280,000 blacks who had registered for the primary. Either large numbers of blacks failed to vote, or many of those who did voted for Waller rather than Evers, or both. (Waller had promised to place qualified blacks in his administration.) Evers not only failed to manipulate black voters in the primary, he was also singularly unsuccessful in retaining their bloc support for his own candidacy.

Manipulation of the electorate is not a characteristic of French presidential elections either. The 1962 runoff pitted De Gaulle against Mitterand of the Left Federation. Based on the findings of French public opinion polls, one student of French politics writes: "Between the two ballots (candidate preferences having been clearly established already), television viewers spent little time listening to candidates not of their choice. After the first ballot, former supporters of defeated candidates quickly made their choice between De Gaulle and Mitterand." The 1965 election runoff was between Pompidou, a Gaullist, and Poher, a Centrist. Prior to the first ballot, it was believed that the Communists would endorse Poher in the runoff if Duclos, the Communist candidate, were eliminated on the first ballot. He was, but the anticipated shift in Communist support was exploded when the Communist party leadership avowed that it saw little difference between Pompidou and Poher, and called on its members to abstain from voting in the runoff. However, "*Le Monde* estimates that the Communist party's demand for abstention was rejected by approximately one-fourth of the Communist electorate and that perhaps 1,200,000 of its voters cast for Poher."[8]

If the relatively highly disciplined French Communist party cannot control all its voters, there is little reason to believe that parties indigenous to the United States can. This appears to be the case even in elections in which the electorate is more concerned with personalities and party than with issues. In the almost issueless election of 1956, Eisenhower's landslide reelection was attributed primarily to personality appeal. But Eisenhower could not deliver his own voters to Republican candidates for Congress while the nation was still predominantly Democratic. Despite Eisenhower's endorsement of fellow Republicans, the Democrats not only retained their majority in Congress in 1956, they increased it.

The low probability that a minor party candidate could sell his popular vote in a runoff also must be balanced against the higher probability that he could deliver his pledged electors if no one wins an Electoral College majority. After the 1968 campaign, "it was revealed that Wallace had obtained written affidavits from all his electors in which they promised to vote for Wallace 'or whomsoever he may direct' in the electoral college."[9] The alternate opportunities for third parties are cogently compared by William Gossett of the ABA:

A candidate rarely, if ever, is able to deliver a block [*sic*] of voters who supported him. On the other hand, he often can deliver the electors; and that is exactly what George Wallace wanted to do and apparently was prepared to do had a deadlock occurred. There would seem to be little incentive for the creation of third parties when they know they have no chance of winning—that the maximum product of their effort would be to require a run-off election; and in any such election, they would have little or no control over those who voted for them. Negotiation for the votes of electors and behind-the-scenes bargains on that level are quite feasible; but dickering for the support of the general public is quite another matter.[10]

The relative disadvantage of minor parties in a runoff would be increased in proportion to their number and degree of political opposition to each other.

Several politically divergent, possibly antagonistic minor parties would be unable to coalesce into a united front, with a united bloc of popular votes to offer a major party. Consequently, their bargaining position, singly and collectively, would be considerably weaker than that of a single third party candidate holding a regionally-based balance-of-power in the Electoral College or in the House of Representatives.

The foregoing analysis of bargaining politics may be summarized by the following propositions:

1. Any bargains struck between the first ballot and the runoff would have to be made public if they were to significantly affect the distribution of the vote in the runoff.

2. Because their electoral constituencies are essentially moderate, both major parties would be unable to accede to extremist demands without losing more votes than they gain. Consequently, presidential elections would not become radicalized.

3. While either major party would be advised to augment its electoral coalition by making concessions on moderate demands (those not considered reprehensible by a majority of the major party's electorate), this act would undermine the viability of moderate minor parties by removing their reason for being. But even failing the demise of moderate minor parties, their continued existence would not radicalize presidential elections (anymore than the Liberal and Conservative parties have radicalized New York politics).

4. Given that minor parties cannot deliver their voters to candidates those voters oppose, or effectively order all their voters to abstain from voting if they do not wish to abstain, only two possibilities are open to minor parties. Either they cannot bargain efficaciously with either major party, or they are constrained to bargaining only with the major party whose issue positions are already closest to those of the minor party. In the former situation, bargaining is precluded and the voters make up their own minds immediately after the first ballot, as in the 1965 French presidential election. In the latter circumstance, since there is only one major party to approach, it follows that the substantive terms extracted from the bargain will be limited. When there is only one buyer, the price the market will allow is low. Again, as in the second proposition, the consequence is that presidential elections would not become radicalized.

5. The fractionalized popular vote of ideologically opposed minor parties constitutes a less valuable bargaining prize in a runoff than do the electors or House members loyal to a single third party candidate under the status quo.

Those who fear bargaining express a degree of panic far in excess of its justification.

Other Aspects of Illegitimacy

Discounting the venality of bargaining by its improbability undercuts, to a degree, three other aspects of illegitimacy attributed to direct election. However, theoretically these aspects can exist independently of bargaining between the first ballot and the runoff, so they deserve separate attention. They are:

1. A "minority" president would be elected if the candidate who comes in second on the first ballot were elected in the runoff. Such a President would have a questionable mandate to govern, and the mandate would be even weaker if there were a lower voter turnout in the runoff than in the first ballot election.

2. Even election on the first ballot could produce a "minority" President; one whose 40 percent plurality means he was rejected by 60 percent of the voters. And he might be elected because of his position on a single issue. Either of these conditions constitutes too narrow a mandate to govern.

3. Election by a 40 percent plurality invites secret deals *before* the first ballot. A major party whose first ballot plurality would be less than 40 percent if a minor party were running would bargain with that party to keep it from entering the election. The other major party would secretly encourage that minor party to run on the first ballot. The minor party would make its decision on the basis of which of the major parties offered the most attractive inducements.

Let us consider these arguments in turn.

Runoffs and Minority Presidents

If the runner-up candidate on the first ballot should win in the runoff, we are warned that this would constitute election "of the candidate who is the second choice of most of the voters." The consequence would be to undercut the President's mandate, weaken the Presidency, and even threaten the stability of the system itself.

The issue at hand is whether a second place finisher on the first ballot who wins the runoff is a "second choice" President. Senator James B. Allen of Alabama makes a superficially strong case that he would be.

Senator Allen hypothesizes a first ballot distribution of the popular vote among four candidates as follows:

Candidate A	39.0%
Candidate B	21.0
Candidate C	20.5
Candidate D	19.5

The runoff would be between A and B. Since A is the front runner, Senator Allen assumes the other candidates all oppose him " and would band together in the runoff and could very likely cause the election of the 21-percent candidate. So that under this plan we would certainly end up with the second choice of the American people being elected as President of the United States."[1]

The more likely situation is that the three trailing candidates could not coalesce against A, in which case A would likely win the runoff. But even if they did manage to unite to elect B, he can be called a "second choice" President only with heavy qualification. The rationale for these statements is as follows:

Given that A is but a scant 11 percentage points from an absolute majority, and given that B, C, and D divide the remaining 61 percent of the vote almost equally, Senator Allen is correct in saying that B, C, and D—and more importantly, their respective voters—would have to "band together" to elect B in the runoff. Assuming B keeps all his own voters, to be elected he would also need either *all* of C's voters *and* a majority of D's voters, or he would need huge majorities of both C's and D's voters. However, either of these combinations would be possible *only* if B, C, and D were ideologically closer to each other than any of them is to A. How likely is that in the real world of politics? Especially when opponents of direct election assume that it would encourage minor parties of both the right and the left? Suppose A is Richard Nixon, B is George McGovern or Edward Kennedy, C is George Wallace, and D is Hubert Humphrey. While Humphrey's voters *might* vote for McGovern, a large proportion of Wallace's voters would not. Many would vote for Nixon in the runoff as their second choice to Wallace, and help elect Nixon.[12] Using the same four-way distribution of the first ballot vote, try any other combination of four candidates, providing it includes candidates both to the left and the right of the two major parties in the center. The results would be the same. The first ballot front runner would win the runoff. He would have enough first and second choice votes to equal a majority of all voters.

Now consider the politically implausible situation of a runoff in which B *does* defeat A because B, C, and D all *do* have more in common with each other than any of them have in common with A. To make this less abstract, let A be Nixon, B be McGovern, C be Kennedy, and D be Humphrey. If McGovern, Kennedy, and Humphrey voters band together to elect McGovern in the runoff, then clearly McGovern is preferred by a majority of voters over Nixon *in the runoff*. In the four-candidate situation of the first ballot, Nixon was admittedly the first choice of a larger percentage of voters than was McGovern, but when the number of available candidates decreases to two, the voters whose first choice is out of the running have to choose from among the secondary choices that are still available. *This is nothing new.* The two-party system presents voters with this situation all the time. The only difference is, the early winnowing process takes place in major party conventions or primaries instead of general elections.

Yet, curiously, when the two parties present the voters with a choice of only two candidates (a Hobson's choice, according to some), this is the salvation of the Republic. If the voters do it themselves, it suddenly becomes the ruination of the Republic.

There is another critical consideration that will be developed below. If A, the leader on the first ballot, is defeated by B in the runoff, then on the first ballot most C and D voters must have ranked B no higher than their second choice, but *they ranked A no higher than their third choice.*[13]

Having accomplished Senator Allen's purpose by electing B, we now see that if B is "the second choice of the American people," it is only because *a majority of the voters do not have a first choice*. Even 40 percent do not have a first choice. Inferences: (1) This fracturing of the vote reflects a preexisting fracturing in the political system. The vote is effect, not cause. (2) In this condition of dissensus, the first choice of even a large plurality (40 percent) cannot be elected because he does not exist. But because the purpose of a democratic election is to elect the available candidate most preferred by the most voters, in this condition that would be the candidate who is the first *or* second choice of a majority of all voters. (3) The runoff accomplishes this purpose, *regardless of whether it is won by the first- or second-place finisher on the first ballot.*

The third inference can be illustrated with the earlier examples. If the front runner A wins the runoff with his first choice 39 percent of the vote plus most of D's 19.5 percent who consider A their second choice, A clearly has a majority over B's 21 percent first choice votes and C's 20.5 percent who favor B as their second choice. Now the second example. If B is elected in the runoff, he does so because he adds to his 21 percent first choice voters at least three-fourths of the combined 40 percent of C and D voters who consider him their second choice and A their third choice.

If one is entertaining the nagging suspicion that something is ethically wrong in a system in which the first choice of 39 percent of the voters loses to someone who is first choice of only 21 percent, consider the alternative. To insist that A "should be" elected instead of B is to insist that the President should be the first choice of 39 percent (A's voters), at best the second choice (and more likely the third choice) of 21 percent (B's voters), and unquestionably the *third* choice of 40 percent (C's and D's voters). Since the C and D voters prefer B to A, it is reasonable to assume that had B not made the runoff, B's voters would prefer C or D in a runoff with A. That is why A is most likely also the third choice of B's voters, as well as of C's and D's. This means that if A were President, he would be the *first choice of 39 percent* and the *third choice of 61 percent*.

One can make one's own decision as to whether this would be ethically preferable to the election of B, who would be the first choice of 21 percent, the second choice of 40 percent, and *at worst*, the third choice of A's 39 percent.

To sum up, Senator Allen's model is vulnerable when his abstractions, A, B, C, and D, become empirically realistic candidates representing actual ideological positions. The model's premises may be valid only for two of America's political processes, and then only occasionally. One process is preconvention and convention politics, when several candidates for a party's nomination might combine to attempt to stop the front runner from winning the nomination on an early ballot, opening the way for a compromise candidate or even a dark horse. But the possibility of several candidates still in the running after many convention ballots is far different from a second, and final, runoff election in which only the top two candidates on the first ballot appear.

The Allen model might also be an accurate representation of some cases of issueless, job-oriented, multi-factional southern primaries. Candidate B might court the support of C and D by promising them patronage, financial payment, or both. But, again, no one claims that multi-party presidential politics would be free of issues. Quite the contrary.

In a variation on the "minority" President theme, Sayre and Parris also surmise that with direct election more people would be unwilling to accept the election results if their favored candidate loses. This would result from more parties and more emphasis on turnout raising the intensity of political conviction. The trouble with this hypothesis is that it doesn't happen when it should. Elections do not bring mass disgust or insurrection in democracies which have much higher voter turnout than the United States—Japan, Israel, England, Italy, France, and West Germany, to name a few. Note, too, that many of these nations have multi- or modified multi-party systems. Also, scholarly research finds that the strongest Republican and Democratic identifiers are the people who are most likely to vote and who have the firmest political convictions and the greatest interest in politics. Yet strong Democrats accept the election of Republican Presidents, and confirmed Republicans pay their taxes to Democratic administrations.

The broader implication of the Sayre-Parris hypothesis is that as the intensity and variability of political demands increase, the number of alternatives from which the public can democratically make its final choice should decrease. *In effect, this says that democratic procedures are bankrupt in those situations when they are most needed.* Just as the First Amendment is invoked only in cases of suppression of unpopular opinion, a democratic electoral system is required most when people disagree about the course of government. As Scammon sees it, the Electoral College is undemocratic in a three- or four-way election. In the old days, he observes, government programs came after the election. Now programs are at issue before the election. To the extent this means the nation no longer has all shades of political opinion neatly collected into a two-party system, the one-stage Electoral College could give the nation a minority President. For this reason, Scammon favors the Bayh proposal with the runoff contingency.[14]

Confusion about the principles of a free election is implicit in such statements as the following: "Undoubtedly, the aura of legitimacy would be all the more in doubt where the runner-up in the initial contest wins the runoff by wooing third-party support. In such a case, the question of legitimacy is sharpened even further if the turnout in the second election is substantially lower than in the first election."[15]

The secondary issue of turnout can be deferred for the moment, for the principal charge has implications raising more questions of legitimacy than it settles. To say that the second place candidate should not win the runoff with the help of minor party voters implies either that such voters should not vote in the runoff, or that if they do, they should not be allowed to freely choose between the two alternatives available. But a vote without choice is not a vote. In short, a first ballot vote for a minor party candidate becomes, in effect, a philosophical justification for disenfranchisement in the runoff election. This violates two fundamental canons of legitimacy in democratic elections, universal suffrage and free choice.

An example can illustrate the problem. Suppose the front runner is Spiro Agnew, the second place candidate is Edward Kennedy, and the minor party eliminated on the first ballot is an ultra-liberal Democratic splinter group led by, say, the Rev. Jesse Jackson. To argue that the first ballot Jackson voters should not be allowed to help elect Kennedy on the second ballot is to say that stray sheep should not be allowed to rejoin their original flock, but must either forego all further rights as sheep, i.e., Democrats, or join a herd of goats by voting for Agnew.

A second implication is that the front-runner candidate might be allowed to win the runoff with the support of minor party voters, but the runner-up candidate should not. The distinction between the legitimacy of the former and the illegitimacy of the latter is unfathomable. To respond that neither of the top two candidates should solicit minor party votes is to suggest that minor party demands should be completely ignored by both major parties, regardless of their substance. That would give the nation a *de facto* two-party dictatorship.

The third implication is that those who voted for the first and second place candidates on the first ballot would be locked into staying with their original choices in the runoff. Although this is highly probable, other things being equal, other things are not always equal. If, for example, there were two minor party candidates eliminated on the first ballot, one liberal and one conservative, the front runner might seek the support of one of those minor parties as assiduously as the runner-up would court the votes of the other minor party. But if the front runner makes concessions perceived as too extreme by his first ballot followers, some of them might switch to the second-place candidate in the runoff. In this situation, it is possible that the runner-up would win the runoff with the help of some former supporters of his opponent, as well as with minor party votes.

All three implications can be summed up to say that unless there is freedom for the voters to elect the second-place candidate in the runoff, it is not truly a democratic election. And if it is not, one might as well elect as President the candidate with the highest plurality on the first and only ballot, regardless of how small that plurality may be.

The foregoing helps put the secondary issue of turnout in its proper perspective. But even considered in isolation, the importance of turnout is minimal or nonexistent. Let us skip the knotty problem of operationally defining when turnout in a runoff is "substantially lower" than in the first election. Assuming consensus on that, we should note that were it not for those minor party voters willing to switch their support to one of the remaining candidates, the runoff would have an even lower turnout. But for minor party voters who favor the second place candidate, a necessary condition for their participation in the runoff is the knowledge that their votes may help elect him. Therefore, to lament low turnout and simultaneously condemn a condition that increases it is egregious.

Generally speaking, if an election is based on universal suffrage, offers some degree of choice, and is decided by an honest count, a low turnout reflects the political satisfaction, dissatisfaction, malaise, or apathy of people *who choose not to vote*. But this is self-imposed political exile. Those who do not vote are voluntarily foregoing a right which is exercised by those who do. For this reason, *the legitimacy of an election's outcome centers on the choice of those who vote, not those who abstain*. Under these conditions, the issue of turnout as an index of legitimacy is a red herring.

French presidential elections demonstrate this. The 1965 runoff between De Gaulle and Mitterand polled 2.5 percent fewer valid notes than were cast in the first ballot. In the 1969 Pompidou-Poher runoff, the drop in valid votes between the first and second ballots was a whopping 16.2 percent. The French did not consider one election more "legitimate" than the other, although De Gaulle's candidacy in the 1965 contest made it more stimulating. That probably minimized the drop-off in votes.

These elections suggest that turnout varies directly with how important it is to the voters which candidate wins. If this hypothesis is valid, then if a second-place candidate wins a runoff with a markedly low turnout, it may be because large numbers of nonvoters don't care which of the two finalists is elected. That is hardly a condition prompting widespread cries of illegitimacy. Neither candidate would enter the White House with the cheers of multitudes ringing in his ears. Conversely, if a second-place candidate wins a runoff with a high turnout, then the low turnout/legitimacy argument is, again, irrelevant.

First Ballot Winners as Minority Presidents

Even if there were no runoff, the "Minority" President charge is leveled at any candidate who might win on the first ballot with less than an absolute majority of the popular vote. A President elected with only 40 percent of the vote, warns Senator Goldwater, is a man who was turned down by 60 percent of the voters.

He may also, write Sayre and Parris, have a narrowly-based, one-issue constituency, such as a Democrat who wins by promising urban dwellers he will save their decaying cities, a Republican who appeals to suburbanites chafing under taxes or inflation, or concerned about law and order, or a candidate who wins 40 percent of the vote solely on the peace issue. "The actual support for such a President might prove to be shallow; his coalition might extend no further than the issue on which he was elected." In short, the direct vote proposal would eliminate "the President's solid mandate to govern. . . . "

The argument withers under examination. Admittedly, a President who wins 40 percent of the electorate has also lost 60 percent. But it has been demonstrated above that in a multi-party situation in which no candidate has majority support, the winner will inevitably be the first choice of only a minority of the voters. Indeed, *minority Presidents have been elected 15 times under the Electoral College*. That the Electoral College may dissuade certain types of minor party candidates from running more frequently than they do is beside the point. When only two major party candidates face each other, the winner's majority is automatic. Consequently, even a "majority" President is not necessarily the first choice from among all possible candidates, but only between the two in the election. A majority of 50.1 percent does not, in and of itself, make the President a tribune of the people.

Conversely, a plurality approaching a 40 percent low does not automatically condemn the President as a usurper, rejected by the people and unable to govern. Wilson carried but 41.85 percent of the popular vote in 1912, yet he conducted an activist administration that had popular support. Nixon won a lowly 43.42 percent of the popular vote in 1968, and the Democrats again won the Congress. This did not inhibit him from proposing many new departures in domestic and foreign policy, and carrying through on several of them.

The first Nixon administration (among others) also flatly contradicts Senator Ervin's charge that a President elected with a 40 percent plurality would likely have the support of not more than 40 percent of the people when he is inaugurated, and that his initial support would diminish month after month until he is supported by considerably less than 40 percent.[16] In fact, a President's popular support after his inauguration is invariably greater than his popular vote in the preceding election. The evidence is found in the monthly Gallup polls which ask a sample of the public whether it approves or disapproves of the way an incumbent is handling his job as President. Compare Nixon's unimpressive 43 percent of the popular vote in 1968 to the 59 percent of the public which approved his handling of the Presidency in January, 1969, the 61 percent who approved in February, and the 63 percent who were favorable in March.

This is typical. Since the Gallup organization began surveying presidential popularity in 1937, *every President has begun a new term of office with a sizable majority of public support, regardless of how he fared in the election*. Call it a honeymoon period or a halo effect, the pattern is clear. The President is legitimized by his office, not by the size of his vote.

A minority President with a mandate to govern on one issue but no other is pretty far-fetched. For one thing, the "mandate" of a presidential election is far from explicit. When the President's party remains in office, the electorate has done very little more than register sufficient satisfaction with existing conditions. It is also a vote of confidence in the in-party's past behavior and an act of faith in its ability to deal with the future.[17]

But even when it is "time for a change," the particular parameters of change usually are not spelled out during the campaign. For one thing, too specific an enumeration of future policy could cost any candidate some votes. Note McGovern's retreat, in 1972, from his original proposal of a thousand-dollar-a-year per person minimum income for the needy. More importantly, *conditions—or judgments about them—may change after the inauguration*. Roosevelt's 1932 campaign promise to balance the budget was not kept. Nor was the vast scope of the early New Deal mapped out in the campaign. Nixon labeled his policy to end the Vietnam war "secret" during the 1968 campaign. He was elected largely because the public believed a new face might be able to do something about a chronic problem in Southeast Asia. But what Nixon would do, or how he would attempt to do it, was unknown, perhaps even to Nixon.

In addition to the vagueness of their mandates, elections rarely, if ever, turn on a single, discrete issue. While a politician may catapult into national prominence on a single issue (Vietnam was the springboard for McGovern, integrated schools for Wallace), candidates for presidential nominations invariably broaden their appeals. Thus, in the 1972 primaries, McGovern and Wallace took positions not only on Vietnam and school busing, but also on welfare and tax reform, the economy, the size of the defense budget, and amnesty for draft-evaders and deserters. To these issues, the general election campaign added the Watergate Hotel bugging affair.

Since it is manifestly improbable that 40 percent of the electorate would favor a candidate's stand on one issue but oppose and/or be indifferent to his positions on all other issues, the likelihood of a "minority" President also being a "one-issue" President is, to be generous, remote. And in the improbable circumstances that an election turns exclusively on a single issue, the President would have a mandate on the only issue that mattered to the public. Since such an issue would have to have universal importance and be universally beneficial, e.g., reducing inflation or unemployment or keeping the nation at peace, the winning candidate would probably receive a majority of the popular vote. He would not be a "minority" President.

Bargaining Before the First Ballot

Although election by a 40 percent plurality is intended to minimize the probability of a runoff, there is a body of opinion which favors a runoff if no candidate receives a majority on the first ballot. This view has been expressed by

Senator Baker, who supports the Bayh proposal, and by Senator Eastland, who opposes it. Senator Eastland presents an interesting reason for his position.

Senator Eastland's argument draws heavily on his scenario of the critical role of minor parties *before the first ballot* if it could be won with a 40 percent plurality. Suppose, he suggests, that a poll taken in the spring of a presidential election year shows that, in a two-party race, the prospective Republican nominee would receive 52 percent of the vote and the prospective Democratic candidate 48 percent. Suppose also that the same poll showed the following vote distribution in a three-way race with a splinter candidate: the Democrat, 44 percent; the Republican, 43 percent; the splinter candidate, 13 percent.

"It should go without saying," Senator Eastland then says, that leaders of the Republican party would "do everything legally and honorably possible to persuade the splinter party candidate not to enter the field," while Democrats would strongly encourage him to run.[18] The leaders of both parties would make secret promises and commitments to the splinter party candidate about future policies and appointments. The splinter candidate would make his decision on the basis of the relative inducements forthcoming from each party. Should he hurt the Republicans by deciding to run, the Democrats "might also be compelled to arrange for considerable campaign financing of the splinter party candidate."

Senator Eastland admits that under his proposed election by majority vote, deals and promises can be made prior to the runoff to obtain the support of minor party candidates.

However, the great difference between the two situations is that in the runoff under the 50-percent system, any deals would be open deals openly arrived at. By the nature of things the entire voting public would know about any effort of one of the two candidates in the runoff to obtain the support of certain groups. Any promises made to these groups to obtain their support would be public promises designed to attract their support.[19]

Conversely, election by 40 percent opens a much greater possibility of "secret wheeling and dealing" before the first ballot.

Except for transposing the popular vote percentages (and, therefore, the victor) between the major party candidates, Senator Eastland's "hypothetical" situation bears a striking resemblance to the 1968 election, and to what might have happened in 1972 had Wallace not been disabled. This lends it an aura of credibility. Certainly those who might not hold President Nixon in high esteem could imagine him trying to keep George Wallace from running by "secretly" making all kinds of "southern strategy" policy concessions, perhaps even by promising Wallace an appointment as Secretary of Health, Education, and Welfare. (Whether Wallace would want such a post is another matter. It *would* be a good position for firing all the "pointy-headed bureaucrats" Wallace condemned in his 1968 campaign.)

However, even those who opposed Humphrey in 1968 or McGovern in 1972 might be hard-put to seriously conceive of either of them encouraging Wallace's states' rights candidacy, no less depleting the minimal Democratic campaign chest by making under-the-table grants to Wallace's campaign. Politics may make strange bedfellows, but a secret Humphrey-Wallace or McGovern-Wallace liaison verges on the politically obscene. Without restricting the argument to particular personalities, the same conclusion would hold with respect to any moderate liberal *vis-à-vis* a conservative minor party candidate, or any moderate conservative who would have to court a liberal splinter candidate. *From this perspective*, the Eastland scenario rests on the premise that any splinter candidate's demands are about equidistant, politically, from both major party candidates, yet close enough to both so that both would at least consider bargaining with him. The validity of the premise is highly questionable.

However, the premise of equidistance is unnecessary for Eastland's thesis if one deduces it from a different set of assumptions: that a Democratic liberal on civil rights, such as McGovern, *would* encourage a Wallace-type candidate to run because (1) the liberal would perceive this act as a precondition to his own election, and victory takes precedence over principles, and (2) since the bargaining would be secret, the public would not know that the liberal had "sold out" his principles. By and large, these tacit assumptions must underlie the Eastland thesis if we are to accept it as tenable.

The unanswered, and unanswerable, question is how tenable are the assumptions? Both presume a degree of cynicism and opportunism in major party presidential candidates that is common in political novels and television dramas, but which may be more a matter of literary license than of empirical evidence. No one is denying a power drive within men who aspire to the Presidency. But short of convincing evidence to the contrary, one may also assume that the Presidency is sought after for reasons of public policy as well as personal ambition. The Presidency is a means through which men can effect the course of a nation. To assume that candidates would bargain away their issue positions to the point of reversal or revocation is to assume that a major motivation for seeking the prize is nonexistent.

Moreover, Senator Eastland would have us believe that such amoral and possibly dysfunctional bargaining will commence solely on the basis of very early soundings of possibly uncrystallized public opinion. As stipulated by Eastland, the poll would be conducted in the spring of an election year—well before the realities of intra-party coalition formation are tested in the nominating conventions and well before any party has even begun its general election campaign. Although the hypothetical spring poll indicates a three-way race would result in a 44 to 43 percent Democratic advantage, the actual election might well reverse these figures. Not only is the one point difference well within the bounds of chance sampling error (as would be a four or five point spread in a typical national sample of 1,500 to 3,000 respondents), but early poll findings showing one candidate the victor "if the election were held today" are often reversed in later polls, on election day, or both. Politicians are not likely to forget 1948 or the close races that developed *during the campaigns* in 1960 and 1968. By encouraging a third party candidacy in spring, the Democratic candidate might be cutting his own political throat in November.

The Eastland thesis also assumes that a major party candidate who consummates a bargain could be confident that his "sellout" would remain secret. Although the chance of secrecy is considerably greater before the first ballot than prior to the runoff, it is by no means absolute. One cannot assume that the news media would not unearth any leaks from political insiders, in both the major and the minor party, who were either privy to the deal or who suspect it had been made. Certainly one source of unkept secrecy would be within the following of the minor party candidate, as exemplified by the situation facing George Wallace in late 1971. Some of his staff and supporters in Alabama did not want him to run for the Presidency in 1972, while many conservatives in other states who had backed him in 1968 wanted him in the race at the head of a full third party ticket.[20] Thus, regardless of which decision the potential splinter candidate makes—to run or not to run—he will disappoint, and possibly embitter, some of his followers. At the least, he would presumably be required to confide in them the reason for his decision, e.g., the provisions of the deal he had made. And as the circle of deception widens, the chances of maintaining secrecy diminish. Especially if the deal which prompted the decision were insufficiently persuasive to those in his entourage who disagreed with the decision.

Nor is a major party candidate a man alone. Those in his party who knew of the deal, and who might resent the concessions made, would be a second source of security leakage. Even if the deal were publicized in the guise of unconfirmed rumors or speculation (a not unknown practice in the news media), it would hurt him. A major party candidate would spend much of his effort denying allegations that he could neither disprove nor admit. That, too, is a not unknown practice in American politics.

On balance, Senator Eastland may be recommending the right course for the wrong reasons. Requiring an absolute majority for election has some appealing aspects to those who do not contemplate minor parties with hysteria. For one thing, the actual vote polled by minor party factions on the first ballot is a far more accurate measure of their popular support than the leaders of such factions claim during primaries, conventions, and in the general election. It might be quite healthy if, for example, a neo-isolationist peace group or an ultraconservative group had to put up or shut up in a general election. If their respective followings proved to be quite small, this would serve to moderate the political scene. At the least, their flamboyant rhetoric could be ignored. If their first ballot strength were sizable, both major parties would be on notice that large segments of public opinion are moving ahead of them and that they had better catch up or do a better job of educating minor party voters about the error of their ways. In either situation—a small minor party vote or a large one—democracy would be served.

Even if minor parties forced the election to a runoff, the final decision would be made between the two top candidates. That preserves the *essential* principle of two-party competition. Finally, if a majority vote could only be achieved through the runoff contingency, that would permit those who voted for minor parties on the first ballot to reappraise their wants in terms of their next best choice—an option that would not be available if a 40 percent plurality were sufficient for election.

Notes

1. Bargaining in southern Democratic primaries is used as a point of departure by Alexander Bickel, REFORM AND CONTINUITY (New York: Harper Colophon Books, 1971), 25, by Wallace Sayre and Judith Parris, VOTING FOR PRESIDENT (Washington, D.C.: The Brookings Institution, 1970), 75-76, and by Professor Ernest J. Brown, visiting Professor of Law at the University of Pennsylvania, in his testimony during the Hearings before the Senate Judiciary Committee on ELECTORAL COLLEGE REFORM, 91st Cong., 2nd Sess. (April 15, 16, and 17, 1970), 120. This latter source will be cited hereafter as Senate Hearings.

2. Testimony of Congressman William Clay of Missouri in Senate Hearings, 68, 70. Clay's fears are echoed with approval in the minority views in Senate Report No. 91-1123, 91st Cong., 2nd Sess., Judiciary Committee, "Direct Popular Election of the President" (August 14, 1970), 41-42. Hereafter cited as Senate Report.

3. Senate Report, 16.

4. See the discussion in Robert A. Dahl, A PREFACE TO DEMOCRATIC THEORY (Chicago: University of Chicago Press, 1956), 96-98.

5. Gerald Pomper, ELECTIONS IN AMERICA (New York: Dodd, Mead, 1968), 154. This paragraph draws upon and extends Pomper's discussion on pp. 153-154.

6. 116 CONG. REC. S15136 (daily ed., September 10, 1970).

7. Ibid.

8. Lowell Noonan, FRANCE: THE POLITICS OF CONTINUITY AND CHANGE (New York: Holt, Rinehart, and Winston, 1970), 454.

9. POLITICS IN AMERICA (3rd ed.; Washington, D.C.: Congressional Quarterly Service, May 1969), 81.

10. Senate Hearings, 194.

11. 116 CONG. REC. S16475 (daily ed., September 24, 1970).

12. See the report of the Gallup poll, as published in THE SUNDAY PANTAGRAPH (Bloomington, Ill.), November 7, 1971.

13. If D voters considered candidate C their second choice, then B would rank as their third choice and A as their fourth choice. Similarly, C voters might prefer candidate D to candidate B, and candidate B to candidate A. But to forego unnecessary complications, the discussion will assume that the two candidates in the runoff rank no lower than the second or third choice of all minor party voters. In a relative sense, this is no different than if they ranked third or fourth, since only two candidates remain for which a vote can be cast.

14. Comment by Richard Scammon during a roundtable discussion, "What Kind of Majority—'Republican,' 'Real,' 'For Change,'—or None?" held the evening of September 10, 1971, at the 67th Annual Meeting of the American Political Science Association in Chicago, Illinois.

15. Separate views of Senators Robert Griffin and Joseph Tydings, in Senate Report, 16.

16. 116 CONG. REC. S16554 (daily ed., September 25, 1970).

17. V.O. Key, Jr., POLITICS, PARTIES, AND PRESSURE GROUPS (5th ed.; New York: Thomas Y. Crowell, 1964), 526ff.

18. 116 CONG. REC. S15136 (daily ed., September 10, 1970).

19. Ibid.

20. CONGRESSIONAL QUARTERLY WEEKLY REPORT, October 30, 1971, 2221-23.

A Mélange of Other Charges

Opponents of direct election do not lack for originality or variety in the arguments they muster. What remains are the red herrings, the mini-arguments which lack the political profundity of those dealt with with deservedly more attention in earlier chapters.

These other charges are that direct election will engender electoral fraud and time-consuming recounts, require complete federal administration of presidential elections, tatter the fabric of federalism, and replace the national convention with a national primary. Failing all else, the final warning is that a direct election amendment would not be ratified by three-fourths of the states.

Fraud and Recounts

Journalist and author Theodore White contends that the Electoral College minimizes the incidence and effect of fraud in presidential elections. Under the present system, White argues, states are self-sealing containers. Any dishonest voting or vote-counting that may occur is limited to a very few states with both a large electoral vote and a close popular vote (e.g., Illinois in 1960). But had direct election been in effect in the close contests of 1960 and 1968, fraud might have run rampant even in such "honest" states as Minnesota, Connecticut, California, and Oregon. "Under direct election," White warns, "a premium would be placed on stealing every vote in every precinct in every state."[1]

The corollary is that because the electoral vote is counted by state, the present system removes the incentive for the party which loses a state to demand a time-consuming recount. For example, in most cases it would make no difference whether there is a question of irregularity about 400 or 500 votes in a few precincts in Austin, Texas. Since the President-elect usually wins proportionally more electoral votes than popular votes, the national electoral vote would probably not be close enough to make any difference which party wins the Texas bloc of electoral votes. Consequently, there would be insufficient reason to demand a recount of a few hundred votes in Austin. On the other hand, even if the national electoral vote were very close, if the party which won Texas' electoral votes carried the state by a landslide, again a few hundred votes would not matter enough to warrant a recount. In sum, this compartmentalization theory of the Electoral College is that (1) fraud is localized to a few states and (2) the electoral votes of these states would not change the outcome of an election; therefore, (3) losing presidential candidates do not insist on recounts.

What if the national popular vote were close in a direct election? Then, the theory continues, recounts which changed a few hundred votes in each of many states, or which changed a few thousand votes in a few states, would be critical. It wouldn't matter whether a statewide vote were close if the national vote is. Charges of fraud in one state, county, or precinct would be met with countercharges of fraud in other jurisdictions. The recounts would escalate in scope, possibly take months to complete, and conceivably leave the nation without a President on the day of inauguration.

Even if fraud were not charged, a close election on either the first or second ballots would entail time-consuming recounts. The elapsed time between the first ballot and the runoff would prolong the period of uncertainty. And if one or more candidates came close to the 40 percent plurality needed for victory on the first ballot, a winner still could not be declared until the total number of votes cast were known. This number might be determined by absentee ballots; again, political leaders would be tempted to demand recounts.

Fraud

The major flaw in the compartmentalization theory is its second premise: that a few thousand fraudulent votes in a few states could not affect the outcome of an election under the Electoral College. Because the unit rule delivers a state's electoral votes in a bloc, quite the contrary is true. As Senator Marlow Cook of Kentucky observed of the 1960 election in California, a change of 25,000 popular votes would have shifted 40 electoral votes. California's 40 electoral votes equal 7 percent of all electoral votes, but 25,000 popular votes equal 0.000385 percent of 65 million popular votes. In 1948, Truman's popular vote plurality exceeded two million. But a change of less than 9,000 votes in California and some 3,600 votes in Ohio—less than one-fifth of 1 percent of the nation's popular vote—would have elected Dewey in the Electoral College. Similarly, a switch of but 11,874 popular votes in five states in 1960 would have given Nixon a majority of the Electoral College and the Presidency.

The principle is clear. As Senator Cook cogently observes, fraud is encouraged or discouraged by its likely impact on an election. And because the change of a few votes in each "insulated state" can shift large blocs of electoral votes, while a few thousand changed votes would be of miniscule importance in a statewide or nationwide pool of millions of votes, *the impact of fraud is magnified under the present system.* In sum, compartmentalizing electoral votes by state breeds the very effect it is alleged to discourage.

What of Theodore White's allegation that direct election would corrupt previously "honest" states, would result in nationwide fraud? Senator Cook properly terms this charge a *non sequitur.* Certainly everyone knew, *before election day*, that the 1960 contest would be close in both popular and electoral votes. Why, then, does White assume such states as California, Minnesota, and Oregon were honest in a close election under the Electoral College but would have been corrupted in a direct election? In 1960, California's 32 electoral votes were won with a plurality of less than 36,000 votes; Minnesota's 11 electoral votes were carried by a 22,000 vote plurality; and Oregon's 6 electoral votes were delivered with a plurality of less than 41,000 votes. In all three states the vote was close enough to make fraud appealing to fraudulent men, *had there been any.*

Moreover, in Senator Birch Bayh's opinion, local politicians are less likely to think the presidency is worth cheating for than the office of sheriff, county commissioner, or governor—positions which dispense patronage. A case in point is the celebrated 1960 election in Illinois. Kennedy carried the state by fewer than 9,000 votes. The day after the election Republicans charged that Mayor Richard Daley's Democratic organization had "stolen" the election in Chicago. The chief Republican purveyor of this charge was Benjamin Adamowski, the Cook County state's attorney. A long-time adversary of Daley's, Adamowski himself lost reelection in 1960 by 25,000 votes. The Republicans demanded and received a recount at their expense. In the words of Mike Royko, from his hostile biography of Daley, *Boss*:

In nine hundred precincts in which paper ballots were still used, the recheck caused a switch of ten thousand votes, narrowing Adamowski's margin of defeat to fifteen thousand.

Nixon gained very little in the nine hundred precincts, showing clearly that the Machine was more concerned with beating Adamowski than electing Kennedy. [2] (Emphasis added.)

Recounts and Delays

In addition to the futile Chicago recount, there was a recount in Hawaii in 1960. However, it was not instigated by the Republicans, but by the courts. Nixon appeared to have won the state's three electoral votes by a margin of 141 votes. The recount found Kennedy the victor by 115 votes.

These episodes of 1960 illustrate a historical pattern. Although the cost of recounts is relatively low (compared to campaign expenditures), and a change in a few thousand votes in two or three states could alter the outcome of close elections, *losing presidential candidates do not ask for recounts.* Nor, except for exceptionally close elections, do statewide candidates. The reason for this disinclination to challenge election results is probably a fear of negative reactions by the voters in the contested election and in future ones. Americans disdain sore losers. As a spokesman for the American Bar Association put it: "If presidential candidates have for 180 years passed up recounts involving only a few states, why are we concerned with the risk of recounts that would involve all fifty states, with doubtful results?"

The infrequency of recounts notwithstanding, those which do occur are both administratively feasible and can be conducted rapidly. The spreading use of electronic voting systems, as well as voting machines, not only diminishes the possibility of fraud or error inherent in paper ballots, but assures speedy counts and recounts.

The allegation that recounts bring delays is vehemently denied by Clay Myers, the Oregon Secretary of State in 1970. Oregon's first statewide recount was in the 1968 U.S. Senate election between Robert Packwood and Wayne Morris. The only delay, writes Myers, was statutory, to certify the first election result, to allow time for a recount demand, and for posting bond. "The total time to actually recount was very brief—even including the certification by all the counties of the recount results, and Senator Packwood had no trouble taking his seat before Congress convened. . . . [I] t is possible to recount hundreds of thousands of votes in five days. We count that number every election."[3]

Myers offers unqualified assurance that there will be a President on the day of inauguration. Even if there were a runoff election on the first or second Tuesday of December (allowing up to a month between the first and second ballots), more than another month would elapse before an inauguration. In Myers' opinion, Congress need make only minor statutory changes in the date the states make the final determination of their election results.

Federal Administration of Elections

Opponents of direct election contend that its adoption will inevitably lead to direct and complete federal administration of presidential elections. Congress would have to adopt uniform standards of voter eligibility and uniform legislation insuring that all candidates would be on the ballot in every state. Both the fear of fraud and the "logic" of a national popular vote count would dictate a centralized, national canvass of the vote, perhaps beginning with federal election officials in every one of the nation's 180,000 precincts.

In any practical sense, these fears are without foundation.

The direct vote proposal provides that qualifications for voters shall be the same for voting for President as for voting for the most numerous house of a state legislature, except that a state legislature may prescribe less restrictive residence requirements and Congress may establish uniform residence qualifications.[4] Congress has already done so, and more. Legislation adopted in 1970 limits residency requirements to no longer than 30 days for presidential elections, abolishes literacy tests in all states, and sets the voting age at 18.[5] Uniform standards of voter eligibility is no longer an issue.

The proposal further provides that the times, places, and manner of holding elections, and *the criteria for placing candidates on the ballot*, shall be prescribed by the legislature of each state. However, at any time Congress may make or alter such regulations by law. In terms of practical politics (Congress is not disposed to easing the birth trauma of minor parties), as well as by the expressed intent of proponents of direct election, this reserve power of Congress would be used only in those cases where states attempt to keep major party candidates off their ballots. This happened to Lincoln in 10 states in 1860 and to Democratic candidates in Alabama in 1948 and 1964. Otherwise, advocates of direct election recommend that states continue to have primary responsibility for including the names of candidates on their ballots.

Their sentiments are the same with respect to the states retaining their function of counting and certifying the vote. Granted, the direct election proposal states that "The Congress shall prescribe by law the time, place, and manner in which the results of such elections shall be ascertained and declared."[6] While this language gives Congress *carte blanche*, a federally administered election is envisioned *only* by opponents of direct election. Its advocates see Congress' role as setting minimal standards for an honest canvass of the vote and a deadline date by which the states shall submit their final, certified count. But within these broad guidelines the states would be given a wide latitude in developing their own laws affecting registration of voters, control of the polling places, and counting and recounting the vote.

The Mystique of Federalism

Few defenses of the Electoral College (and attacks on direct election) rest on such empirically unsubstantiated myth and intellectually arid symbolism as the federalism theory. In its narrowest sense, the theory contends that both small states and large derive disproportionate political leverage from the College. In its more sweeping pronouncements, the theory imputes an intangible but philosophically important quality or character to popular majorities pressed through the sieve of the Electoral College.

Large States and Small States

"Many political leaders in small states," write Sayre and Parris, "view the general ticket [unit rule] as serving their interests, because with two electors based on their equal representation in the Senate, they have a greater percentage of the electoral college vote than of the popular vote. And many political leaders in populous states believe that the system serves *their* interests because of their large blocs of electoral college votes."[7]

The leverage that large states are supposed to derive from the Electoral College is more shadow than substance. As Gus Tyler points out, the large states do not unify into a decisive bloc of electoral votes because in *close elections* they divide and cancel each other out. In 1948 and again in 1968, the eight largest states split evenly—four going Republican, four Democratic. In every close election of this century, 1916, 1948, 1960, and 1968, writes Tyler, the five largest states have split three to two.[8]

The theoretical advantage of small states is also largely mythical. Not having common interests, such states do not vote as a bloc. The District of Columbia is not likely to follow the lead of North Dakota or Rhode Island the lead of Idaho.[9]

By contrast, the strong regional continuity of southern states prompts them to vote more or less cohesively. Selective historical disenfranchisement of blacks has reinforced this regional homogeneity. More importantly, it has contributed to the South's consistently having a voter turnout far below the national average and even farther below the turnout of nonsouthern states. The South's cohesion at the conservative end of the spectrum on selected issues and *its historically low popular vote compared to its electoral vote* is what Tyler calls the "Dixie Edge" in the Electoral College. It explains, writes Tyler, why there have been repeated southern movements for a third party to throw the election into the House of Representatives, why George Wallace almost succeeded in his 1968 venture, and why the southern strategy has a special appeal to some of Nixon's political advisers. Tyler concludes that "The politicking for the present system revolves around on amoral axis. The big state pols believe the present system favors them; the small state pols believe it favors them; the low vote state pols *know* it favors them." (Emphasis added.)

Tyler's analysis is corroborated by the fact that the most cohesive opposition to direct election emanates from southern political leaders. Southern cohesion is exemplified in the two unsuccessful attempts to close debate on the direct vote proposal (S.J. Res. 1) in the waning days of the 91st Congress. Southern Senators (those from the 11 states of the old Confederacy plus Kentucky and Oklahoma) were far more unified in preventing a vote on the proposal than were Senators from small states (those with 8 or fewer electoral votes).

On the first cloture attempt, 20 of 26 southern Senators voted against ending debate, while small-state . . . Senators split almost evenly: 25 for cloture, 21 against, and 6 not voting.
On the second cloture attempt, 20 of 26 southern Senators again voted against ending debate, while small-state Senators split evenly: 23 for, 23 against and 1 not voting.[10]

As Peirce observes, another reason "that 'overrepresentation' of a state is an illusory advantage is that the people of a state do not vote unanimously for one Presidential candidate or another—although the unit vote system of casting electoral votes may make it look as if they had. But it is *people* who have preferences, not states."[11] The point is well taken. Nevada's three electoral votes grossly overrepresent its population. In 1960 those electoral votes went to Kennedy. The small "state" advantage was, in reality, an advantage to the 54,880 Nevadans who voted for Kennedy at the expense of their 52,387 fellow citizens who voted for Nixon.

Qualitative Majorities

Here is a riddle. According to opponents of direct election, when is a majority vote for President not a majority vote for President? Answer: When it is not a "reasonable" majority—one that respects the rights of others. "The central character of American politics requires that we be concerned not just with the *size* of majorities but with their *character.*"[12]

This sentiment, expressed by Senators Eastland, McClellan, Ervin, Hruska, Fong, and Thurmond, is the old concurrent majority principle in thin disguise. It should therefore be no surprise that four of the six Senators subscribing to these words represent the South, as did John C. Calhoun. Yet prior to the adoption of the Voting Rights Act of 1965, the "character" of voting majorities in much of the South was small in size, white in race, and not very "reasonable" in respecting the rights of black citizens.

But the grand mystique of federalism is by no means restricted to southern Senators. A northern liberal, Richard Goodwin, expresses similarly curious views about the nature of American democracy. As he rightly observes, the federal government is not constituted along the lines of the pure democracy of a town meeting. The Supreme Court is accountable to no electorate, although it can overrule both the Executive and Legislative branches, which are. The Senate is numerically undemocratic in composition but currently is the most progressive and liberal branch of all. And a powerful President can appoint Attorneys General and Secretaries of State who, themselves, have more power over the destiny of the people than most of our early Presidents. "And so," says Goodwin, "to determine if a structure or process is democratic we ask *not how many decide and in what manner*, but whether it adds to oppression or increases freedom, confines opportunity or enhances the general welfare, fragments the union or perfects it. By that standard, the electoral college is not undemocratic."[13] (Emphasis added.)

In point of fact, the only way to determine whether a "structure or process" is democratic is to ask the very questions that Goodwin rejects: how many decide and in what manner? As questions about procedures, they are legitimate inquiries into the *form* of government. But Goodwin commits the generic intellectual error of many of the self-styled "liberals" of the late 1960s and early 1970s. He defines "democracy" principally in terms of the *substance of public policy*. The key question of democracy is no longer how many people can control the selection of their leaders, but what the leaders do for the people.

What is wrong with that? Everything. In terms of the logic of democratic theory, Goodwin's thesis leads to the *reducto ad absurdum* that the one-man, authoritarian regime of a "benevolent" dictator is democratic. (But only, of course, for those citizens who receive the benefits.) Far more importantly, in the day-to-day political arena, Goodwin's definition of "democracy" is no longer ideologically neutral. Terms like "oppression," "freedom," "opportunity," and "union" mean quite different things to Goodwin, William F. Buckley, Jr., George Wallace, and Eldridge Cleaver. Or, for that matter, to Francisco Franco and Fidel Castro. To define democracy as Goodwin does is to risk escalating disagreements over public policy into conflict over the far more critical question of the structure of American government. That is the essence of radical politics of both the left and the right.

Nor are Goodwin's references to the "undemocratic" branches of government relevant. No proponent of direct election wants Senators, Supreme Court justices, and members of the Cabinet elected by the nation-at-large. Just the President—who *appoints* judges, secretaries of state, and attorneys general—and who therefore should be responsible to all the people for his appointments.

Popular election of the President would leave unscathed the *genuine* protection of pluralistic interests inherent in our federal system. In contemporary practice, the House of Representatives remains the repository of local interests while the Senate protects the interests of states, as such, and is the principal safeguard of our federal republic. But the Presidency has evolved as the sole elective office responsible for the overall national interest to the citizenry as a whole, much as the federal courts are the legal bulwark of both the public interest and the procedural and substantive rights of individuals. Moreover, any President—whether elected by "reasonable" or "unreasonable" majorities—will remain subject to the checks and balances of two legislative chambers and the Supreme Court. The Bill of Rights no more rests on the Electoral College than does the pork barrel.

The creed of American federalism is *"E Pluribus Unum"* ("Out of Many, One"). Nowhere is the practical application of this slogan better expressed than in the words of Tom Wicker: "We may be 50 states in Congress but we are one people in the White House—or should be—and the President ought to be ours to choose."

National Primaries

Opponents of direct election insist that it will destroy the political power of state party organizations, for the "logic" of direct election leads to replacing the nominating convention, composed of state party delegations, with presidential primaries that would probably be national in scope. To Professor Ernest J. Brown, this portent approaches the immutability of natural law: "If you have direct popular election, the nominating procedure must necessarily follow in some way the election procedure. If there were such a thing as electoral physics, I would be tempted to put this as a law of physics."[14] We would probably have, Brown concludes, a nationwide primary for each party.

Professor Brown's statement is an assertion, not a validated empirical generalization. As a matter of "logic," there is no reason whatsoever why a national convention cannot nominate a candidate who will be directly elected. Institutions of nomination are quite independent of electoral institutions, as exemplified by France, where Presidents are elected by the people but not nominated by them. American nominating conventions would continue to be composed of state party delegations because that is an administratively and politically convenient way to organize them, just as the counting of general election ballots in the states is administratively convenient.

There are also cogent political reasons to retain the nominating conventions. A strong champion of direct election, Neal Peirce, mentions a few of them:[15]

1. The convention is a forum in which disparate elements of the party can reach the compromises needed to agree on a party platform.

2. Since the convention nominates both the presidential and vice-presidential candidates, there is a natural pressure to select men who can run on the platform and a subsequent pressure on them to live up to the broad principles enunciated in it.

3. The party professionals who attend the convention are aware that their nominee must appeal not only to strong partisans, but to independent voters as well. Independents would presumably be excluded from the party's nominating primary. The experienced, professional judgment of party "pols" in picking a man who appeals to independents is of no small consequence. As V.O. Key concluded from his study of state primaries, the strongly partisan voters may nominate a man too much in their own image; one who pleases rabid Democrats or Republicans voting in their respective primaries but who has insufficient support to carry a majority in the general election.[16]

4. There may be cases when none of the candidates for nomination has built a really broad base of national support. In these circumstances (admittedly rare), the convention can "draft" candidates, such as Charles Evans Hughes in 1916 and Adlai Stevenson in 1952.

5. If both presidential and vice-presidential candidates were elected in a nationwide primary, the men chosen to run together might represent sharply antagonistic points of view or even be antagonistic toward each other. However, this contingency could be obviated by allowing the presidential candidate to choose his own running mate, as is present practice.

In sum, good politics as well as good logic dictates retaining the nominating convention. Nominations are for parties; elections are for voters. "Rather than the electoral college, the conventions should be recognized as an institution that produces a 'concurrent majority' in American Presidential politics."[17]

Ratification by the States

A constitutional amendment requires approval by a two-thirds vote in each house of Congress and ratification by three-fourths (38) of the states. Would an amendment to replace the Electoral College with a direct vote muster the necessary support from legislatures in the smaller states? Or would their opposition prevent a three-fourths majority from being reached? Not being gifted with prescience, we cannot offer a definitive answer. The question is raised only because opponents of direct election claim it would not be ratified, but the available evidence suggests that it might.

In the summer of 1969, Senator Robert Griffin of Michigan conducted a mail questionnaire of all the state legislators in the 27 smallest states. Forty-four percent of those questioned responded, and of these, 64 percent endorsed direct election. In only two of the 27 states was there less than a majority who said they would vote to ratify a direct election amendment. The Griffin survey corroborated the findings of an earlier poll conducted by Senator Quentin Burdick of North Dakota in the summer of 1966. Burdick wrote to the 8,000 state legislators in all the states and received answers from 2,500 of them. Fifty percent or more of the respondents in 44 of the 50 states supported direct election of the President and 58.8 percent of all state legislators endorsed the proposal. The Burdick poll showed almost equal support for direct election from small states as well as from medium- and large-sized states.

While the Griffin and Burdick polls do not make ratification of a direct vote amendment a foregone conclusion, they are impressive empirical indicators for two reasons. First, both polls offered legislators alternative proposals to direct election, such as retaining the Electoral College, the district plan, and the proportional plan. Given the number of options which could fractionalize the response, the absolute majority for direct election is even more impressive. Second, the surveys were conducted before an amendment had even passed Congress and been sent to the states. Consequently, the proposal had not acquired the degree of public notoriety and popular support that may be expected when (and if) the states are presented with an amendment. While there is little doubt that there will be strong lobbying against, as well as for, direct election, given the overwhelming popular support for the proposal recorded in Gallup polls, it seems safe to surmise that an even larger number of state legislators will vote for an actual amendment than supported a hypothetical one.

Notes

1. Quoted in Senate Report No. 91-1123, 91st Cong., 2nd Sess., Judiciary Committee, "Direct Popular Election of the President" (August 14, 1970), 42. Herafter cited as Senate Report.

2. Mike Royko, BOSS: RICHARD J. DALEY OF CHICAGO (New York: New American Library Signet Books, 1971), 124.

3. Letter, Clay Myers, Oregon Secretary of State, to Senator Birch Bayh, September 4, 1970, printed in 116 CONG. REC. S15780-15781 (daily ed., September 17, 1970), at the request of Senator Mark Hatfield of Oregon.

4. H.J. Res. 681, 91st Cong., 1st sess., sec. 2, and S.J. Res. 1, 91st Cong., 2nd sess., sec. 2.

5. PL 91-285, 84 Stat. 314 (1970).

6. H.J. Res. 681, 91st Cong., 1st sess., sec. 4, and S.J. Res. 1, 91st Cong., 2nd sess., sec. 4.

7. Wallace Sayre and Judith Parris, VOTING FOR PRESIDENT (Washington, D.C.: The Brookings Institution, 1970), 64.

8. The states are New York, Pennsylvania, Ohio, Illinois, and California. These paragraphs draw heavily on the brilliant analysis in Tyler's written statement published in the Hearings before the Senate Judiciary Committee on ELECTORAL COLLEGE REFORM, 91st Cong., 2nd Sess. (April 15, 16, and 17, 1970), 217-218. Hereafter cited as Senate Hearings.

9. True enough. But there is a tendency for the really small states—defined as those with four or fewer electoral votes—to go disproportionately, if not unanimously, Republican in close elections such as 1960 and 1968. In 1960 there were 15 small states with a total of 54 electoral votes. Ten states with 37 electoral votes went to Nixon, five states with 17 electoral votes were won by Kennedy. There were 16 small states in 1968 with 58 electoral votes among them. Twelve states with 43 electoral votes were won by Nixon, four states with 15 electoral votes were carried by Humphrey. However, (1) not only is the total electoral votes of such states relatively small, but (2) the electoral votes of small states won by Democrats come close to wiping out the "constant two" electoral votes advantage of the small states that went Republican. On balance, Tyler's argument stands, if with qualifications.

10. CONGRESSIONAL QUARTERLY WEEKLY REPORT (April 23, 1971), 944. The four senators from the border states of Kentucky and Oklahoma split three to one in favor of cloture on both motions. The dissenter was John Sherman Cooper of Kentucky. If Kentucky and Oklahoma are excluded from the definition of the South (leaving only the 11 former Confederate states), and Oklahoma (with its eight electoral votes) is defined as a small state, the cohesion of the South is even more manifest. On the first cloture attempt, 19 of 22 southern senators voted against ending debate, the three dissenters being Baker and Gore of Tennessee and Yarborough of Texas, while small state senators divided 27 for cloture (including Harris and Bellmon of Oklahoma), 21 against, and 6 not voting. On the second cloture vote, the distribution among southern senators was the same as on the first, and small state senators split 25 for cloture, 23 against, and 1 not voting. Note that CONGRESSIONAL QUARTERLY has included in its "vote" pairs for and

against, and senators who announced their position or declared their position in a CONGRESSIONAL QUARTERLY poll, even if they did not actually cast a yea or nay vote on the floor. These categories of "vote" included but a few senators, and are certainly reasonable in the light of the main purpose—to plumb political sentiment on this issue. (See CONGRESSIONAL QUARTERLY WEEK-LY REPORT, issues of September 18, 1970, 2240 and September 25, 1970, 2349 for first cloture vote, and the issue of October 2, 1970, 2396 and 2429 for the second cloture vote.)

11. Neal R. Peirce, THE PEOPLE'S PRESIDENT, (New York: Simon and Schuster, 1968), 263.

12. Minority views in Senate Report, 29.

13. Goodwin's testimony in Senate Hearings, 86.

14. Testimony in Senate Hearings, 122-123.

15. Peirce, PEOPLE'S PRESIDENT, 268-269.

16. V.O. Key, Jr., AMERICAN STATE POLITICS: AN INTRODUCTION (New York: Alfred A. Knopf, 1966), 152-165. It is important to note that Key's conclusions are based on a primary electorate which is small in number and unrepresentative of the larger population of party identifiers.

17. Peirce, PEOPLE'S PRESIDENT, 269.

Part III
Recommendations

7

Where Do We Go From Here? And Why?

Rationality may be defined as a careful delineation of one's goals or values as a prerequisite to determining the most expeditious manner of achieving them. In more common parlance, if you don't know where you want to go, you won't know how to get there.

Disputations arise because men (1) seek incompatible goals, (2) agree on common goals but differ over the means to achieve them, (3) define a common goal so imprecisely that there is consequent confusion over the means to reach it, or all three. If the preceding pages have accomplished nothing else, they should have demonstrated that the manner of electing the President is not a final goal over which men disagree; rather, the electoral system is considered an instrumentality or means for achieving other, more valued ends. To the extent these ends or goals are clearly incompatible, e.g., seeking political influence disproportionate to their number for citizens of one group of states versus equalizing political influence for all voters nationwide, the conflict is irreconcilable.

Much of the preceding analysis has attempted to remove this first cause of conflict by empirically demonstrating the falsity of one of the conflicting goals. We have argued, for example, that the Electoral College does not bestow special advantages to the urban residents of large states or to the citizens of small states, but only to some of the voters of some southern states. Similarly, we have attempted to undercut the conflict between the goal of one man, one vote and the goal of insulating major party candidates from bargaining for minor party support by contending that minor parties would be unable to compromise the integrity of major party candidates.

Nonetheless, it would be self-deluding to assume that every opponent of direct election who reads these pages will change his mind. To the extent a goal has become an *idée fixe*, even the most intelligent person clings to it. And it must be admitted candidly that arguing by inferential reasoning leaves legitimate areas of disagreement, for both the data from which inferences are drawn and the inferences themselves may be open to question. Therefore, no further effort will be expended on attempting to reconcile incompatible goals. Instead, these final comments will be devoted to explicating a set of goals on which, hopefully, a high level of consensus can be reached, and to removing the remaining two causes of conflict—differences and confusion over the means of achieving them. These goals are the components or criteria of an ideal presidential election system.

Criteria of an Ideal Presidential Election System

Senate proponents of direct election have submitted three criteria of a "modern electoral system." It should (1) guarantee that the man with the most votes is elected, (2) count each vote equally, and (3) provide the people themselves with the right to make the choice. Predictably, the conclusion is that only direct election meets all three tests.[1]

Unfortunately, these criteria are self-serving. They are clearly intended to make direct election the only, inevitable means for reaching them. Consequently, the criteria are too limited; they do not encompass at least two other values which legitimately may be required in an electoral system: a quick decision about who the winner is, and at least benign neutrality toward, and preferably outright support for, the two-party system.

Another set of criteria, which encompasses those of the Senate proponents and the two respecting quick decisions and the two-party system, were agreed to by a conference of experts (identity undisclosed) assembled by The Brookings Institution in February 1969. These criteria will be submitted here as the goals of an ideal presidential electoral system upon which consensus should be possible. As set forth by Sayre and Parris, the criteria are as follows:

Four criteria, some of which tend to conflict, were accepted by the conferees as components of an ideal system for electing the President and Vice President:

First, the election procedure should guarantee, insofar as possible, a quick election decision with a clear-cut winner. The possibility of a period of "constitutional crisis," during which the identity of the victor is uncertain, should be eliminated or at least minimized.

Second, the system should be democratic. "The people's choice," the man with the most popular votes, should win.

Third, the President should be "legitimate," as defined by twentieth-century conceptions of democracy in the United States. He should have a margin of votes sufficient to be generally considered a "popular mandate to govern." Precise parameters of legitimacy have never been established. An acceptable mandate is a margin of victory somewhere between a *plurality* of one vote and a *majority* of one vote.

Finally, the system should not undermine accepted norms of American politics, particularly the two-party system.[2]

It is our contention that, contrary to Sayre and Parris's appraisal, these criteria do *not* "tend to conflict" when implemented by direct election. Rather, disagreement by the experts over what electoral system would best serve these goals is the consequence of differences over means to achieve them and imprecise and/or unnecessary definitions of a goal, with a consequent confusion over means. The case for this contention will be argued in a series of observations about the criteria.

We observe, first, that the first criterion, a quick decision with a clear-cut winner, is assured only if an election is won handily with a comfortable majority (or plurality) of popular votes. And the size of the majority or the plurality is a function of the voting behavior of the electorate, not of the form of the election. Failing a majority or plurality of significant size, even the Electoral College does not eliminate or "at least minimize" a "constitutional crisis." As has been demonstrated in the preceding pages, the appearance of a clear electoral vote majority is deceiving in an election with a close popular vote. A change of a few thousand votes in one or two states with a large bloc of electoral votes could swing an electoral vote majority from one candidate to another. Secondly, a regionally-based third party, or slate of unpledged electors, could cause a "constitutional crisis" by denying any candidate an electoral vote majority. Finally, if an electoral vote majority should be won by a candidate who comes in second in popular votes, that candidate might be a "clear-cut winner" in the Electoral College, but unquestionably there would be a "constitutional crisis" in the ethical sense, with the identity of the "real" victor challenged by those who believe it should have been the popular vote winner, in conformity with the second criterion.

To sum up the first criterion, it is more likely to be violated by the Electoral College system, *qua* electoral system, than by the direct election system, *qua* electoral system. *No* "election procedure" *can* "guarantee . . . a quick election decision" *in a close election*. The quickness of the decision will depend on the rapidity of counting the vote and, if necessary, recounting it where, when, and if challenged. This rapidity is a function of voting machines, electronic ballot scanning and computer counting, and so on. These technical aspects of canvassing the vote are independent of the electoral system itself.

The second observation is that, given the third criterion, the second is redundant and, therefore, unnecessary. Both criteria say that the candidate with the most popular votes should win. The third criterion simply points out that there is no agreement on what is meant by "the most," although it is "somewhere between" a one-vote plurality and a one-vote majority. We may dispense with the second criterion as unnecessary underbrush and focus on the problems left in operationally defining the third and fourth criteria.

The third observation is that a precise meaning of the third criterion, legitimacy, must be decided upon as a prerequisite to establishing the structure of a presidential election. Should the President win with a plurality or a majority of the popular votes? Sayre and Parris inform us that only a few of the experts supported "a one-shot, winner take-all *popular plurality* contest. Those who did argued that the popular verdict could be rendered decisively, with no possible recriminations that the 'real' popular favorite had somehow lost in a second contest." Many other experts, however, feared that the winning plurality would be far too low—perhaps well below 40 percent—with a consequent impairment of the President's legitimacy and mandate to govern.

We have already dealt with, and hopefully discredited, the argument that "the real winner" would lose if the leader on the first ballot lost the runoff. We also agree that electing a President with too small a plurality is a disservice to the nation, to democratic principles, and to the President-elect. What, then, is too small? Below 40 percent, or below a majority? The first is the criterion used in S.J. Res. 1. The second is that proposed by Senator Eastland and, after considerable reflection, by this writer. If the 40 percent criterion were used, runoff elections would possibly be necessary on some occasions, but not too many. If an absolute majority were required for election, runoffs would be required in an unknown, but certainly more frequent, number of elections.

The criterion of the size of the President's winning vote then becomes a consequence of how one feels about runoff elections. Attitudes toward runoffs are, in turn, a consequence of different perceptions of how to implement the fourth criterion of supporting the two-party system. This is the fourth observation, and it is not merely inferred. Sayre and Parris tell us that, "Indeed, the possible effects of the direct-vote plan on the party system was the central concern of many political scientists at the meeting," and that "There was wide agreement among the participants that popular runoff elections are undesirable, mainly because they encourage minor parties to wage 'spoiler' campaigns." Continuing, Sayre and Parris state: "Many voiced fear that a popular runoff would splinter the political parties. Thus, one political scientist said that minor party leaders would successfully urge many voters to vote their real convictions on the first ballot, since they would have a second choice in the runoff. Most conferees agreed with this analysis." Two or three participants took different positions.

Our fifth observation, then, is that no consensus on the definition of the third criterion, the size of a legitimizing vote, is possible until a precise definition of "two-party system," the central concept of the fourth criterion, is agreed upon. Our sixth and final observation is that even "experts" on the electoral process differed over which electoral system implements the two-party system because, perhaps unknown to themselves, they held different conceptions about the characteristics of a two-party system.

Some of these conceptions fall far beyond the bounds of the conventional definitions of a two-party system, as understood by many political scientists and politicians. Certainly those conferees who condemned popular runoffs because they would encourage minor parties to engage in spoiler campaigns must hold a curious idea of what constitutes a two-party system. Since the only "spoiling" likely is to postpone a victory for a major party candidate from the first ballot to the runoff, we fail to understand the concern. Similarly, the conferee who said runoffs would splinter the major parties because people would vote their "real convictions" on the first ballot *because* they could vote for their "second choice" (presumably a major party candidate) in the runoff is not only assuming a great deal about what constitutes the "real convictions" of most voters; he, too, entertains a one-sided definition of a two-party system.

Both of these concerns can only be based on a "two-party system" defined as one in which minor parties receive very few votes, *regardless of whether only two parties have any chance of winning an election*, as would be the case in a popular runoff. In short, the nearly paranoidal fear of runoffs stems from a definition of party system *which has as its sole characteristic the number of parties winning votes instead of the number of parties winning office*.

We reject this single characteristic for measuring the number of parties in a system as being politically unrealistic. Instead, we offer the characteristics originated by Ranney and Kendall, two political scientists, for creating a five-fold classification of party systems within each of the several states. Their classification is ideal for present purposes, for they were concerned with elections for single offices voted upon in each state—President, Governor, and U.S. Senator. The study is based on elections from the Civil War to 1952, so the references to "votes" and "offices" are in the plural.

The classification scheme, and the characteristics of each class, are as follows:

1. *The Multiple-party type.* To this type belongs any system in which at most elections in the fairly recent past (a) three or more parties have shared the bulk of the votes and public offices, and (b) no single party has won a majority of either votes or offices (so that most governments have been coalition or "fusion" governments).

2. *The two-party system.* To this type belongs any system in which at most elections in the fairly recent past (a) two parties have shared the bulk of the votes and public offices between them, (b) the winning party has gained a majority of the votes and offices, and (c) the two dominant parties have alternated in winning majorities.

3. *The modified one-party type.* To this type belongs any system in which at most elections in the recent past (a) one party has won all or almost all the offices, but (b) the second party, though it has seldom won any offices, has normally received a substantial percentage of the votes and thus constitutes a significant center of organized party competition.

4. *The one-party type.* To this type belongs any system in which at most elections in the recent past (a) one party has won all or nearly all of the offices, and (b) the second party has usually received only a small percentage of the popular votes.

5. *The totalitarian one-party type.* To this type belongs any system in which either (a) only one party has been permitted to participate in elections in the recent past, or (b) any parties other than the dominant single party that have participated are clearly "fronts" for the dominant party.[3]

We assume that all parties to the issue-at-hand will stipulate that, short of abrogating the Bill of Rights, we may remove the totalitarian system from further consideration.

Applying their characteristics to past national elections, both presidential and congressional, Ranney and Kendall conclude that "On the basis of both kinds of data, then, the national party system is clearly of the two-party type." It can be demonstrated that the system will not change into the multi-party type under our proposal—direct election by majority vote with a popular runoff as a contingent election.

The first characteristic of a multi-party system is "(a) three or more parties have shared the bulk of the votes *and public offices* . . ." (emphasis added). Since our proposal insures that a majority of votes must be won, either on the first ballot or, failing that, in the runoff, it follows that only one of the two parties with the two largest popular followings could win the Presidency in any given election, and that one or both of the two most popular parties would win the Office over a series of elections.

The proposal does not, of course, guarantee that the Republican and Democratic parties, as now named and constituted, will continue to be the two major parties in contention. While the Democratic party can trace a virtually unbroken history back to Jefferson's Republican-Democratic party, the Republican party succeeded the Whigs and the Whigs succeeded the Federalists. It would be possible, given severe enough changes in political attitudes, that either or both parties might be replaced by another. But that is beside the point. There would still be only two parties that could contend for the Presidency, and they could only be the two largest parties. The runoff between the top two vote-getters assures this. So does election by a simple plurality on the first ballot, or by a plurality of at least 40 percent. But while the runoff and the 40 percent plurality insure that a President will have a mandate large enough to be legitimate, the simple plurality plan does not.

The requirement that election be by absolute majority has two other consequences that make it superior to election by plurality, whether any-sized or 40 percent. First, it permits voters whose minor party first choices were eliminated on the first ballot to vote for their second choice of major party candidates in the runoff. This not only serves democracy by giving the electorate two opportunities to exercise their preferences, *it strengthens the two-party system by making the two major party candidates the alternatives of last resort.* Second (and this is a corollary of the first consequence), election by absolute majority permits voters to vote for a spoiler candidate if they wish to on the first ballot, but it prevents a spoiler candidate from literally spoiling the chances of a major party candidate with a majority of first *and* second choice votes from winning the election in the runoff. In short, "spoilers" would be unable to spoil. Knowing this, they would be less likely to campaign if this were their only or overriding motive. *Again, the consequence is to strengthen the viability of the two-party system.*

If one wanted to really stretch for a point, it could be argued that, theoretically, three or even four parties could alternate as the "top two" parties from one election to the next; e.g., in the 1976 election the three top parties might finish on the first ballot in the following order: Democratic, Republican, American Independent, while the election of 1980 might result with the top three candidates being Democratic, American Independent, and Republican—in which case the runoff would be between a Democrat and George Wallace or his successor.

The response to this scenario is twofold: First, any political situation this "far out" would also be possible under the Electoral College. If a George Wallace ever reaches the point where he can outpoll one of the major party candidates in a direct election, he likely will be able to do the same in electoral votes. Second, the entire political history of the English-speaking nations (not just the United States) demonstrates that national politics is dominated by only two parties. One of them may be *replaced* by a third party, as happened in Great Britain when the Laborites succeeded the Liberals, but there have not been extended periods when *three parties were of roughly equal electoral strength*. Tradition, the single-member legislative constituency, and (in the United States) the single Executive office all militate against this.

Finally, it is theoretically possible that "three or more parties" could share the "bulk of the votes" on the *first ballot* under the majority vote proposal (depending on how one defines "bulk"). But that matters not, so long as three parties could not share the bulk of victories in achieving the presidential office.

The same arguments demonstrating that direct election by majority vote will not engender a multi-party system simultaneously prove that direct election would be compatible with the three characteristics of a two-party system, *viz.*: "(a) two parties have shared the bulk of the votes and public offices between them, (b) the winning party has gained a majority of the votes and offices, and (c) the two dominant parties have alternated in winning majorities."

The third characteristic requires that both major parties remain as competitive in the future as they have been in the past. If they do not, the country could evolve into either a modified or unqualified one-party type. But since neither proponents nor opponents of direct election expect this, and since, should it occur, it would result from a massive change in public attitudes essentially independent of either direct election or the Electoral College, that realm of speculation lies far beyond the domain of our concerns.

Summing up, on all the criteria of an ideal presidential electoral system:

1. We have precisely defined the characteristics of a two-party system, as required by the fourth criterion.

2. We have demonstrated that direct election by majority vote, with a popular runoff if necessary, is eminently compatible with a two-party system, and may even sustain it in a manner superior to that of election by plurality.

3. Through points (1) and (2) above, we have removed confusion over the best means of implementing the fourth criterion. That is, a popular runoff has been eliminated as a threat to the two-party system, as defined.

4. Elimination of this threat has, in turn, permitted us to define the third criterion of presidential legitimacy as a majority of one. That also serves to define "most popular votes" in the redundant second criterion.

5. At the outset, we demonstrated that the first criterion—a quick, decisive electoral decision—is more a function of the closeness of the vote and the

technical efficiency of its canvass than of the electoral system, but that the Electoral College is, if anything, more likely to cause a "constitutional crisis" over the identity of the winner than is direct election.

Recommendations

If, as is our hope, a consensus can be reached on the four criteria, as defined, as the goals of a presidential election system, and if we have succeeded in removing disputations over the best means of achieving these goals, it but remains to explicitly recommend that means. It is direct popular election of the President by majority vote, with a popular runoff contingency if a majority is not reached on the first ballot.

Second in priority—to be worked for only if the first choice is clearly unattainable—would be direct election by no less than a 40 percent plurality on the first ballot, with a popular runoff between the top two candidates if the minimal plurality is not reached. This would require redefining the third criterion of legitimacy as a 40 percent plurality, but the nation and the Presidency could probably live with that. They have 15 times in the past.

We do not recommend any other option as being worthy of attention at this time, for three reasons. First, the "logical" third choice—election by simple plurality on the first and only ballot—opens too great an opportunity for minor parties, whether spoilers or others, to wreak mischief with electoral choice. Admittedly, most other federal officials are elected by simple plurality, and the absence of viable minor party contestants in their elections gives the winner a *de facto* majority or an exceedingly high plurality. But that is a consequence of public attitudes, not the structure of elections. The ideal electoral system is one that, in the interests of the practical *implementation* of democratic choice as *public policy*, encourages two-party systems and, in the interests of the *aggregation* of democratic choice, permits one or both of the two major parties to be replaced by others more reflective of the public will, as occurred just prior to the Civil War. Election by a plurality of any size does not, in our judgment, meet both these standards as well as election by absolute majority or by a minimal plurality of 40 percent.

Another reason for not offering a third priority, fallback position is that none of those remaining meet all the criteria of an ideal election system. Any of the so-called hybrids, with popular election on the first ballot but not as a contingency, violates the criteria of quickness, democracy (election of the candidate with the most popular votes), or both. A contingency election in Congress violates both criteria, and the schemes which fall back on electoral votes or votes won in a given number of states violate the criterion of democracy.

Practical politics dictate the third and final reason. So long as the nation continues to elect Presidents with majorities or pluralities exceeding 40 percent of the popular vote, *despite* the Electoral College, we are, in effect, achieving our first or second priority. There is no compelling need for changing the present system into something which would give us results *less desirable* than those already recommended. However, on the day the Electoral College goes awry— when it "elects" as President the candidate who polled second place in popular votes, or when a regional party prevents any candidate from winning a majority of electoral votes and the election is decided either by bargaining for minor party electors or in the House of Representatives, with each delegation casting one vote—on that day public opinion will *demand* passage of a direct election amendment.

The near-miss of the 1968 election aroused concern in Congress—enough for passage of a direct vote resolution in the House but not enough to stifle a filibuster in the Senate. But the Electoral College is a sword of Damocles. When it falls, public opinion will insist it be removed forever.

In the meantime, he does not serve who stands and waits. The Senate must be convinced that its duty is to prevent a potential threat from becoming an electoral disaster. For although the Senate will surely act after the disaster, neither party in the Senate will escape the onus of not voting on a direct election amendment when it should have.

Notes

1. Senate Report No. 91-1123, 91st Cong., 2nd Sess., Judiciary Committee, "Direct Popular Election of the President" (August 14, 1970), 9.

2. Wallace Sayre and Judith Parris, VOTING FOR PRESIDENT (Washington, D.C.: The Brookings Institution, 1970), 153.

3. Austin Ranney and Willmoore Kendall, "The American Party Systems," THE AMERICAN POLITICAL SCIENCE REVIEW, 48 (June 1954), 480-481.

Index

Adamowski, Benjamin, 93
Adams, John Quincy, 20
accommodation, 62
administration: federal, 94
age: Wallace voters, 70
Agnew, S., 82
Alabama, 95; 1968, 36; blacks, 39; and
  Kennedy, 10; Longley and Yunker, 34;
  and Wallace, 88
Alaska: Humphrey, 10
Allen, J. B.: runoff, 78
amendment, 100; First, 81; Twenty-Third, 32
American Bar Association, 3, 93; Commis-
  sion on Electoral College Reform, 67
American Nazi Party, 59
Arkansas, 61
Ashbrook, John, 64
Austria, 62

balance of power, 25
Baker, H., and Bayh's proposal, 86; cloture,
  101; inhibition, 11; minor parties, 68
Banzhof, J., 31; unit rule, 8
bare bones, theory of, 64
bargaining: analysis of, 77; opportunities, 9;
  concessions, 71; and Electoral College,
  8; first ballot, 85; and minor party sup-
  port, 55, 105
Bayh, Birch, 3; and Baker, 86; and direct
  election, 14; runoff, 81
Bellmon, H., 101
Bickel, Alexander, 3, 14; direct election, 26;
  malapportionment, 49, 50
Big Eleven: pluralities, 35
Bilbo, T., 61
Birchites, 59
Bischoff, Charles, 9
Black, Charles, 6, 62; and Ervin, 20
blacks: disenfranchisement, 96; and influ-
  ence, 34; and national voting bloc, 39;
  and special leverage, 26
Brookings Institute, 106
Brown, Ernest J., 98
Bryan, William Jennings, 73
Buckley, James, 59
Burdick, Quentin, 100
Byrd, H., 10

California, 101; in 1948, 20; in 1968, 36;
  fraud, 92; hinterland, 30; honest, 91;
  shift, 9
candidate, minority, 5
Catholics, 52; and Democrats, 28

census: federalism, 19
Chamberlain, L., 48
Church, F., 49
citizen-voter, concept of, 32
civil rights, 41, 42; and Ervin, 4; and Truman, 10
Cleveland, G., 8
cloture, 96–101
coalitions, 60; Bickel, 14; conservative, 48;
  decision-making, 14; formation, 53, 72;
  hypothetical, 74; intraparty, 87
committee system, 50
communists, 58
Community Action Program, 43
compartmentalization theory, 91
"compensating effect," 7
Congress: election by, 13; and policy, 25;
  Eighty-Eighth, 48; Eighty-Ninth, 50;
  Ninety-First, 3; Ninety-Second, 4
Connecticut: honesty, 91
conservative: definition, 3
"constant two," 5, 101; in Maine, 20
constituency, 62
convention, 14, 81
Cook, Marlow, 92
Cooper, John Sherman, 101
corruption, 19; unit rule, 12
Cronin, T., 48
cross-pressure, 15
Curtis, Carl T., 3

Daley, Richard: in 1960, 93
deadlock: Bickel, 14
debate: rules of, 50
deGaulle, C., 75; runoff, 83
delegation: state, 9
Democrats, 15; National Committee, 75
Dewey, T., 9; in 1948, 20; switches, 92
direct election: Bickel, 26; urban interests,
  30; vote plan, 108
Dirksen, Everett, 49
disenfranchisement, 12, 82
dissensus, 80
distribution: of vote, 5
district plan, 17
disunity, 60
Dixiecrats, 65–68
Dixie Edge, 96
dogmatism, 58
Dole, Robert, 18
draft laws, 51
dualist theory, 58
Duclos, F., 76
due process: Ervin, 4

115

shifts: Kennedy and Nixon, 10
socialization, 58, 69
Socialists, 58, 63
social welfare, 41
Sorauf, F., 58
Sorenson, T. C., 53
Spenser, H., 11
splinters: candidates, 64; concessions by
    parties, 12; spoiler, 64, 108
spoiler, 64, 108; definition, 66
stability, 55; and runoff, 78
strategy: southern, 96
structures, 108–112; alteration, 17
suburbanites, 30
suffrage, universal, 82
Sullivan, Charles, 75
Swan, Jimmy, 75
swing, voter, 28

Tennessee: plurality, 61
Texas: and close vote, 91; and Democrats,
    30; power, 32; runoff, 64; textbook
    theory, 50
third party, 57
Thurmond, J. Strom, 3, 97; 1948, 10, 20
Tilden, S. J., 8
Truman, H.: 1948, 20; and Dewey, 10;
    plurality, 9, 92
turnout, voter, 19, 81

Tydings, Joseph, 13
Tyler, Gus, 96–101

unit rule: Banzhof, 8; and blacks, 40; and
    direct vote plan, 25; and Electoral
    College, 55; and federal district plan, 19;
    and splinter candidates, 64
urban interests, 25, 49
U.S. Chamber of Commerce, 3, 64

Vermont, 31
Virginia: 1968, 36; Democratic party, 61
volatility: and bargaining, 72
vote: popular, 8–12; eligibility, 94
Voting Rights Act of 1965, 11, 97

Wallace, George, 10, 64; distribution, 79;
    integration, 71; plurality, 38; third-party
    candidate, 15
Wallace, Henry, 67
Waller, William, 75
Washington, D.C., 32; 1968, 36
West Germany, 81
White, Theodore, 3, 91
Wicker, Tom, 98
Wilson, W., 84
Wolfinger, R. and Heifetz, J., 50

Yarborough, T., 101

About the Author

Harvey G. Zeidenstein is an associate professor at Illinois State University. He received his B.S. from Northwestern University, M.A. from the University of Chicago, and Ph.D. in political science from New York University in 1965. From 1961-65 he was a research associate with the Illinois Legislative Council. Professor Zeidenstein teaches courses in American political parties and the American Presidency, and has published articles in these fields in such journals as *The Journal of Politics* and the *International Review of History and Political Science.*